1 MONTH OF FREE READING

at

www.ForgottenBooks.com

By purchasing this book you are eligible for one month membership to ForgottenBooks.com, giving you unlimited access to our entire collection of over 1,000,000 titles via our web site and mobile apps.

To claim your free month visit: www.forgottenbooks.com/free900329

* Offer is valid for 45 days from date of purchase. Terms and conditions apply.

ISBN 978-0-265-85827-1
PIBN 10900329

This book is a reproduction of an important historical work. Forgotten Books uses state-of-the-art technology to digitally reconstruct the work, preserving the original format whilst repairing imperfections present in the aged copy. In rare cases, an imperfection in the original, such as a blemish or missing page, may be replicated in our edition. We do, however, repair the vast majority of imperfections successfully; any imperfections that remain are intentionally left to preserve the state of such historical works.

Forgotten Books is a registered trademark of FB &c Ltd.
Copyright © 2018 FB &c Ltd.
FB &c Ltd, Dalton House, 60 Windsor Avenue, London, SW19 2RR.
Company number 08720141. Registered in England and Wales.

For support please visit www.forgottenbooks.com

REPORT

OF

THE ADJUTANT GENERAL

OF THE

State of North Carolina

1 AUGUST 1951 - 31 DECEMBER 1952

CONTENTS

	PAGE
Report of The Adjutant General 1 August 1951—31 December 1952	5
Report of Audit Year Ended 30 June 1951	12
Report of the United States Property & Disbursing Officer 1 January 1951—31 December 1952	19
Reports of Field Training Calendar 1951-1952 (In Part)	24
Executive Orders 8 and 9 of 1951	34
General Orders (24 thru 40) 1951	35
General Orders (1 thru 34) 1952	48
Certain Special Orders and Letters of Importance and General Interest	92
Total Number Officers & Enlisted Men Who Attended Service Schools 1951-1952	91
Report of Accomplishments of Air National Guard Units While on Active Duty with United States Air Force	104
Rosters: Officers North Carolina National Guard 1951-1952	109
United States Army Instructor and Advisor Personnel 1951-1952	144
Presentation of Eisenhower Trophy 1951-1952	150
Presentation of Third Army Training Trophy 1951-1952	151
Special Duty of Troops 1951-1952 None	152
Former Adjutants General of North Carolina	153

REPORT

OF

THE ADJUTANT GENERAL

OF THE

STATE OF NORTH CAROLINA

FOR THE PERIOD AUGUST 1, 1951—DECEMBER 31, 1952.

To: *His Excellency, The Governor of North Carolina and Commander-in-Chief of the State Military Forces. Executive Office, Raleigh, North Carolina.*

Sir: Submitted herein is a report of the operations of The Adjutant General's Department for the years 1951-1952.

COMMENDATIONS

Several organizations, officers, and men of the North Carolina National Guard have received the commendation of Regular Army and Air Instructors and of the Commanding General, Third Army. Such recognition on the part of Regular Army and Air Officers is evidence of the organization, state of training, and efficiency attained, for which the officers and non-commissioned officers and enlisted personnel are to be congratulated.

Battery B, 113th Field Artillery Battalion at Dunn was awarded the Third Army National Guard Training Trophy for the calendar year 1951. This trophy is awarded to the outstanding National Guard unit in the Third Army Area for each calendar year, based on certain criteria.

The Service Battery, 112th Field Artillery Battalion, Lenoir, was awarded the Eisenhower Trophy for outstanding performance during 1951. This trophy was established in honor of President Eisenhower in 1948 when he was General of The Army, and is awarded each year to the company size Army National Guard unit in each State, Territory, and the District of Columbia on the basis of outstanding performance in training, attendance, weapons qualifications, strength, and other factors.

At the annual armory inspections conducted in the fall of 1952 for fiscal year 1953, there were twelve units which received a rating of SUPERIOR, the highest rating attainable. This is the largest number of units attaining a rating of SUPERIOR in any fiscal year in the history of the North Carolina National Guard. More units received an EXCELLENT rating and fewer units received a SATISFACTORY rating, with no unit receiving an UNSATISFACTORY rating. The North Carolina National Guard is properly proud of this record.

MOTOR VEHICLE STORAGE BUILDINGS

A brief resume of physical properties owned by the State of North Carolina and being used for the benefit of the North Carolina National Guard is considered appropriate for this report. During the years 1949, 1950, and 1951 there were constructed thirty-six (36) motor vehicle storage buildings with funds provided entirely by the Federal Government at a total cost of $857,412.00; an Airplane Hangar at a cost of $14,981.00, and two Satellite Radar Stations at a total cost of $99,366.70. The Federal Government, therefore, has provided $971,759.70 to provide these facilities for the North Carolina National Guard, with the exception of the airplane hangar, all of these buildings were constructed on land donated to the State of North Carolina. Of the motor vehicle storage buildings, thirty-two (32) are being used as armories, and the satellite radar stations are being used to house the 263rd Communications Squadron Operations of the Air National Guard.

ARMORIES

The Congress of the United States for fiscal year 1952 appropriated 24 million dollars for military construction, Reserve Components. This entire amount was allotted for National Guard construction, with 16 million dollars being set apart for armory construction and 8 million dollars for non-armory construction. North Carolina's share for armory construction was $330,817.00. For fiscal year 1953, the Congress appropriated 20 million dollars for military construction, Reserve Components. However, only 8 million dollars of this was allotted to National Guard construction, and of this amount, 5 million dollars was allotted to armory construction and 3 million dollars to non-armory construction. North Carolina's share for armory construction was $105,481.00. This makes a total of $436,290.00 for armory construction.

These armories are based on plans prepared in the National Guard Bureau, with the number of square feet in each item going into the armory determined by the Reserve Components Facilities Board. In order to conform to the building code for public buildings, it was necessary that these plans be redrawn. In so doing, economies of construction were effected which in no wise impaired the usefulness of the building or increased maintenance costs. Bids were received on 18 December 1952 for an armory at Burlington and for an armory at Red Springs. The low bids on the Burlington armory totalled $97,281.00 and on the Red Springs armory $98,513.00. These bids were very much of a surprise to the National Guard Bureau, because it had estimated the cost of construction of these armories at $140,000.00 each. The low bids were approved and contracts for construction were authorized. The National Guard Bureau authorized the advertisement for bids for the construction of an armory at Lenoir, with the interior plan modified to provide for a battalion headquarters and two batteries of artillery.

The cost of construction of these armories is borne by a 75% contribution by the Federal Government and a 25% contribution by the State of North Carolina. If bids on additional armories are in line with the first two, the State will be able to construct six (6) armories instead of four (4) with funds allotted for fiscal year 1952 and 1953.

Armories located as follows and originally built with Federal funds provided through Works Progress Administration in 1935, 1936, 1937, and 1938, augmented by ground and funds furnished by the respective communities, are now the property of the State: High Point, Morganton, New Bern, Parkton, Salisbury, Washington, Whiteville, Wilson, by deed, and Dunn and Roanoke Rapids by twenty-five (25) year leases.

UNITS WHICH ENTERED ACTIVE FEDERAL SERVICE AND THEIR REORGANIZATION

In the preceding Report of the Adjutant General, there is listed the units of the North Carolina National Guard which had been called into active Federal service as a result of the undeclared war in Korea. The 82nd Congress, at its Second Session, enacted Public Law 461, which authorized the President to retain unit organizations and the equipment, exclusive of the individual members thereof, in the active Federal service for a total period of five (5) consecutive years. This law further provided that the Secretary of the Army and the Secretary of the Air Force could, under such regulations as the President might prescribe, provide for the organization of units of the National Guard and the Air National Guard whenever the unit organizations were retained in the Federal service. Pursuant to this law, regulations were issued authorizing the organization of NGUS units bearing the same numerical designation but at reduced strength. The numerical designation of each of the following units was retained in active Federal service: 378th Engineer Combat Battalion, 449th Field Artillery Observation Battalion, 540th Field Artillery Battalion, and 690th Field Artillery Battalion. Authority was obtained to organize NGUS units effective two years from the date of entry on active Federal service of the parent unit. The following NGUS units have been organized:

378th Engineer Combat Battalion (NGUS)

Unit	Station	Date Of Federal Recognition
Headquarters	Charlotte	20 November 1952
Hq. & Service Company	Charlotte	20 November 1952
Company A	Lincolnton	21 November 1952
Company B	Charlotte	20 November 1952
Company C	Statesville	19 November 1952

540th Field Artillery Battalion (NGUS)

Headquarters	Monroe	3 November 1952
Headquarters Battery	High Point	3 November 1952
Battery A	High Point	3 November 1952

Service Battery, Battery B and Battery C not yet organized.

449th Field Artillery Observation Battalion (NGUS)

No units organized.

690th Field Artillery Battalion (NGUS)

No units can be organized until after 23 January 1953.

The 156th Fighter Squadron, Air National Guard, was reestablished at Charlotte on 10 July 1952, and effective that date was redesignated as the 156th Fighter Interceptor Squadron, and was redesignated as the 156th Fighter Bomber Squadron on 1 December 1952.

The Adjutant General's Department was advised that the 118th Aircraft Control and Warning Squadron would not be returned but authorized the organization of the 263rd Communications Squadron Operations, and this unit was extended Federal recognition on 8 October 1952 occupying the radar buildings at Wadesboro and Badin which had been constructed for the 118th Aircraft Control and Warning Squadron.

REPORT OF THE ADJUTANT GENERAL 9

SERVICE SCHOOLS

During the period covered by this Report, one hundred (100) Officers and two hundred thirty-two (232) **EM** had attended Service Schools.

CAMPS OF INSTRUCTION, 1952

During the summer of 1952, the 30th Infantry Division, under command of Major General Paul H. Jordan of Chattanooga, Tennessee, with Brigadier General Claude T. Bowers of the North Carolina National Guard as Assistant Division Commander, engaged in annual field training at Fort McClellan, Alabama. The IV Corps Artillery, the 167th Military Police Battalion, the 3624th Ordnance Company also trained at Fort McClellan. The 252nd AAA Group engaged in field training at Camp Stewart, Georgia, together with the 130th AAA Battalion, a part of the 30th Infantry Division. The training at both installations was most satisfactory and the accommodations all that could be desired.

ARMY INSTRUCTORS

Colonel Lee C. Bizzell, 0-10250, Infantry, was transferred in the summer of 1952 after serving three years in this assignment. He performed his duties in an outstanding manner. He was succeeded by Colonel William R. Watson, 0-8354, Infantry, who took over the duties of Senior Army Instructor in July. Colonel Watson has his office in the Adjutant General's Department. He has shown a deep interest in his assignment and has been energetic in his personal visitations to the units of the Guard at their respective home stations. He and his officer assistants have been especially helpful in counciling and advising with unit commanders, and particularly in assisting them with respect to property. Colonel Watson is a native of North Carolina, served four (4) years in the office of the PMS&T, North Carolina State College, during which time he attended two field training periods with the 120th Infantry. He has a thorough knowledge of the problems of the National Guard and is most energetic in his efforts to assist. His assistants, both commissioned and enlisted, have rendered valuable service and have been most helpful. I wish to record my appreciation of their unselfish devotion to their duties. Especially I wish to commend the Sergeant Instructors in the Office of the Senior Instructor for their very fine cooperation with the Adjutant General's Department and for their interest and efficient work on behalf of the National Guard.

REPORT OF THE ADJUTANT GENERAL

THE UNITED STATES PROPERTY AND DISBURSING OFFICER

Lt. Colonel Michael H. Austell, with former service as an assistant to Colonel Gordon Smith, assumed the duties of the United States Property and Disbursing Officer on 2 October 1947 and continues to perform his duties in a most efficient manner. His knowledge acquired through years of experience and the thoroughness and care with which he handles the many details of his duties are outstanding. His office has handled the many administrative details required to place approximately 50 million dollars worth of clothing and equipment in the hands of National Guard units of this State, all of which has been furnished through the Federal Government. He has to maintain very detailed records and carries on his books approximately twenty-two thousand (22,000) items. His records must show where each item of property is. He has four auditors who make a complete inventory of all property in the hands of each unit once each year, and he must make inventory of the many thousands of items in his three warehouses at Camp Butner. During the past twelve months, over 2 million dollars worth of new motor equipment has been issued, and all of the World War II motor equipment has been turned in. His office makes all contracts for construction which is paid for wholly with Federal funds. He must make the necessary arrangements for the transportation of troops to and from field training, provide for their rations while at field training, as well as the petroleum products required for motor vehicles, and all types of ammunition to be used. His service in every particular has been of the highest order.

STATE MAINTENANCE OFFICER

Lt. Colonel John Foreman is a State Maintenance Officer of unusual and outstanding ability. He has had wide experience in ordnance for many years. The Ordnance Maintenance Shop at Camp Butner is operated under his supervision. It makes repairs to all motor vehicles, weapons, signal, and engineer equipment of the North Carolina National Guard. He makes an annual inspection of all ordnance, signal, and engineer property in the hands of each unit. He is with the Inspection Teams sent out by Third Army through most of their inspections. He handles much work for the Adjutant General's Department, although his compensation is paid with Federal funds.

STAFF AND EMPLOYEES
THE ADJUTANT GENERAL'S DEPARTMENT

The staff and employees of this Department merit the respect and confidence of the State and the Departments of the Army and Air Force. The staff members are officers of experience in the National Guard and World War II. They are efficient and perform their duties with interest and intelligence. Several employees of the United States Property and Disbursing Office and the Adjutant General's Department have many years of service with the Department. It is largely through the efficiency of his staff and employees that the head of a department may effectively perform his duties to the benefit of the State and Federal Governments.

The office space allotted to the United States Property and Disbursing Officer is over-crowded and inadequate. The same is true of the Adjutant General's Section. I urgently request additional office space for the Adjutant General's Department. Additional office space is its greatest need.

GENERAL

I consider the National Guard of North Carolina at this time the best trained and best equipped in its history. On 31 December 1952 it had a total strength of 622 Officers and 5,017 Men in the Army National Guard, and 20 Officers and 155 Men in the Air National Guard. Due to the demands of the Selective Service System, it has been difficult to increase the strength, but the determination of the officers and non-commissioned officers has made it possible to keep its strength from declining. All honor is due to them.

DEPARTMENT OF THE ADJUTANT GENERAL
RALEIGH, NORTH CAROLINA

REPORT ON AUDIT
Year Ended June 30, 1951
General John H. Manning, Adjutant General

INDEX

COMMENTS:

EXHIBIT:

    "A"   Statement of State Appropriated Funds and Expenditures

SCHEDULES:

    A-1   Statement of Departmental Receipts
    A-2   Detailed Statement of Expenditures
    A-3   Statement of Disbursing Account
    A-4   Statement of Salaries and Wages

EXHIBIT:

    "B"   Summary Statement of Comparative Expenditures
    "C"   Statement of Receipts and Disbursements—N. C. Armory Commission

Report of The Adjutant General

DEPARTMENT OF STATE AUDITOR
BUREAU OF INSTITUTIONAL AND DEPARTMENTAL AUDITING
RALEIGH, NORTH CAROLINA

General John H. Manning
Adjutant General
Raleigh, North Carolina

Sir:

We have made an examination of the accounts and records of the

DEPARTMENT OF THE ADJUTANT GENERAL
RALEIGH, NORTH CAROLINA

for the fiscal year ended June 30, 1951 and submit herewith our report consisting of two Exhibits and four Schedules which we believe to be self-explanatory. We also show on Exhibit "C" a statement of receipts and disbursements of the North Carolina Armory Commission. There was an unexpended balance of $171,795.01 at June 30, 1951. This amount was transferred to reserve account for permanent appropriations North Carolina Armory Commission.

Expenditures for the Department of The Adjutant General's office for the year 1950-51 were $309,079.90 compared to $311,011.57 for the previous year, or a reduction of $1,931.67 for the year 1950-51. This was accounted for mainly by the fact that certain units of the National Guard (Air and Ground) were inducted into Federal Service.

We inspected a representative number of invoices, payrolls, and other data supporting disbursements and found them in order. The cash balance at June 30, 1951 was reconciled with the records of the State Treasurer and found in agreement.

We wish to express our appreciation to the personnel of the Department for the courtesies extended us during this assignment.

Respectfully submitted,

HENRY L. BRIDGES, *State Auditor*

Prepared By:

BUREAU OF INSTITUTIONAL AND DEPARTMENTAL AUDITING
By JNO. W. IVES

Approved:

M. L. WIDENHOUSE
C.P.A.

May 16, 1952

STATEMENT OF STATE APPROPRIATED FUNDS AND EXPENDITURES

Year Ended June 30, 1951

May 16, 1952   EXHIBIT "A"

UNEXPENDED BALANCE JULY 1, 1950	$ 0
1950–1951 APPROPRIATION	295,486.00
TRANSFERRED FROM 1949–1950 MAINTENANCE	1,500.00
DEPARTMENTAL RECEIPTS (SCHEDULE A-1)	20,830.68
TOTAL AVAILABILITY	$ 317,816.68
TOTAL EXPENDITURES (SCHEDULE A-2)	$ 309,079.90
UNEXPENDED BALANCE OF APPROPRIATION	$ 8,736.78

REPRESENTED BY:

UNEXPENDED BALANCE AVAILABLE FOR FUTURE USE:

Transfer to 1951-52 Maintenance	$ 1,292.00
UNEXPENDED BALANCE REVERTED TO STATE'S GENERAL FUND	7,444.78
	$ 8,736.78

STATEMENT OF DEPARTMENTAL RECEIPTS

Year Ended June 30, 1951

SCHEDULE A-1

RECEIPTS:

U. S. TREASURY REIMBURSEMENTS:

Camp Butner	$ 6,039.54	
Morris Field	10,445.69	
Bluenthenthal Field	4,345.45	
TOTAL RECEIPTS (To EXHIBIT A)		$ 20,830.68
Refund of Expenditures		652.00
TOTAL DEPARTMENTAL RECEIPTS AND REFUNDS		$ 21,482.68

DETAILED STATEMENT OF EXPENDITURES— MAINTENANCE FUND
Year Ended June 30, 1951
SCHEDULE A-2

ADMINISTRATION:
Salary—Adjutant General	$ 7,920.00	
Salaries and Wages—Staff	48,474.34	
Supplies and Materials	921.75	
Postage, Telephone, Telegrams	3,723.26	
Printing and Binding	2,091.82	
Repairs and Alterations	156.85	
Equipment	2,364.92	
Maintenance State Owned Auto	696.26	
Motor Vehicle Purchase	683.23	$ 67,032.43

NATIONAL GUARD:
Officers Special Duty	$ 6,046.35	
Travel—Adjutant General	654.01	
Allotment to Organizations	125,381.41	
Commanding General, 30th Div.	1,000.00	
Examination of Recruits	16,743.00	
Insurance and Bonding	141.24	
Association Dues	870.40	
State Arsenal—(Freight & Labor)	794.48	
Other Expense	211.86	
Travel—Checking Federal Property	814.82	
Courts Martial	109.00	
Allotment to Officers and Supply Sgts.	54,561.11	
Workman's Compensation	632.00	
Armory Inspections	5,646.92	$ 213,606.60

CAMP BUTNER:
Salaries and Wages	$ 4,555.63	
Materials and Supplies	1,792.41	
Utilities	308.00	
Maintenance and Repairs	563.48	$ 7,219.52

MORRIS FIELD:
Salaries and Wages	$ 3,152.55	
Supplies and Materials	3,298.48	
Communication and Shipping	649.29	
Sub-Contractors	3,600.00	
Utilities	2,654.82	
Maintenance and Repairs	879.56	$ 14,234.70

BLUETHENTHAL FIELD:
Salaries and Wages	$ 4,420.00	
Supplies and Materials	386.25	
Communications—Shipping	177.68	
Utilities	796.58	
Maintenance and Repairs	1,117.86	$ 6,898.37

SPECIAL DUTY:
Raleigh-Durham Airport		$ 88.28

TOTAL EXPENDITURES	$ 309,079.90

STATEMENT OF DISBURSING ACCOUNT
Year Ended June 30, 1951

SCHEDULE A-3

BALANCE JULY 1, 1950	NONE
RECEIPTS:	
From State Treasury (Transfer from allotment account to Disbursing Account)	$311,023.90
TOTAL BEGINNING BALANCE AND RECEIPTS	$311,023.90
DISBURSEMENTS:	
Expenditures (Schedule A-2)	$309,079.90
Transfer to 1951-52	1,292.00
Refunds (Schedule A-1)	652.00
TOTAL DISBURSEMENTS	$311,023.90
BOOK BALANCE JUNE 30, 1951	NONE
RECONCILIATION WITH STATE TREASURER:	
Balance on State Treasurer, June 30, 1951	$ 1,500.70*
ADD: Deposit in Transit	85,000.00
" "	9,045.74
	$ 92,545.04
DEDUCT: Outstanding Checks	$ 92,545.04
BALANCE AS ABOVE	NONE

*Indicates Red Figures

SUMMARY STATEMENT OF COMPARATIVE EXPENDITURES

Fiscal Years Ended June 30, 1951 and June 30, 1950

EXHIBIT "B"

	Fiscal Year Ended June 30, 1951	Ficsal Year Ended June 30, 1950	Increase Decrease*
SUMMARY BY PURPOSES:			
Administration	$ 67,032.43	$ 57,681.26	$ 9,351.17
National Guard	213,606.60	220,522.58	6,915.98*
Camp Butner	7,219.52	5,654.96	1,564.56
Morris Field	14,234.70	21,423.83	7,189.13*
Bluethenthal Field	6,898.37	5,134.78	1,763.59
Special Duty	88.28	594.16	505.88*
TOTAL EXPENDITURES	$ 309,079.90	$ 311,011.57	$ 1,931.67*
SUMMARY BY OBJECTS:			
Salaries and Wages	$ 68,522.52	$ 62,891.36	$ 5,631.16
Supplies and Materials	6,398.89	6,277.48	121.41
Postage, Tel., and Tel.	4,550.23	5,043.32	493.09*
Travel Expense	1,468.83	1,695.16	226.33*
Printing and Binding	2,091.82	1,519.29	572.53
Motor Vehicle Operation	696.26	575.99	120.27
Lights, Power, Water	3,759.40	3,830.36	70.96*
Repairs and Alterations	2,717.75	1,294.23	1,423.52
General Expense	1,082.26	1,348.97	266.71*
Insurance and Bonding	141.24		141.24
Equipment	2,364.92	62.80	2,302.12
Extraordinary	215,285.78	226,472.61	11,186.83*
TOTAL EXPENDITURES	$ 309,079.90	$ 311,011.57	$ 1,931.67*

North Carolina Armory Commission
STATEMENT OF RECEIPTS AND DISBURSEMENTS
Year Ended June 30, 1951

EXHIBIT "C"

UNEXPENDED BALANCE OF APPROPRIATION (TRANSFERRED FROM 1949–50)		$ 173,781.81
DISBURSEMENTS:		
Maintenance and Repairs to Armories	$ 1,505.11	
Deeds and Land Titles	369.50	
Printing	112.19	
TOTAL DISBURSEMENTS		$ 1,986.80
UNEXPENDED BALANCE OF APPROPRIATION		$ 171,795.01
REPRESENTED BY:		
RESERVE ACCOUNT FOR PERMANENT APPROPRIATIONS: North Carolina Armory Commission		$ 171,795.01

REPORT OF U. S. PROPERTY AND DISBURSING OFFICER

SUBJECT: Report of U. S. Property and Disbursing Officer for North Carolina

TO: The Adjutant General
State of North Carolina
Raleigh, North Carolina

1. Report of the U. S. Property and Disbursing Officer for the period 1 January 1951 to 31 December 1952 is hereby submitted.

2. During the period covered by this report, this Office performed the following functions required by law and regulations:

　a. Maintained accountable property records for all technical services property received, issued, and returned to the Department of the Army and Department of the Air Force.

　b. Requisitioned and issued to Units all Army and Air Force property which was required and which was available.

　c. Performed duties of Transportation Officer for North Carolina Army and Air National Guard.

　d. Performed duties as Purchase and Contract Officer where Federal Funds were involved.

　e. Performed all duties as Budget and Fiscal Officer, Army and Air National Guard, for expenditures of Federal Funds.

　f. Drew all Federal property for housekeeping, and that property requested and made available for training, at Field Training Camps and re-issued same to using organizations.

　g. Maintained leave records of and prepared vouchers for salary payments for all employees of the North Carolina Army and Air National Guard.

　h. Performed for the Adjutant General other duties pertaining to the operation of the National Guard.

3a. During the Calendar Years 1951 and 1952, the following Units were organized, recognized, and equipped:

Unit	Location	Recognized
123rd Sig. Radar Maint. Unit, Type C	Wilmington, N. C.	24 Jan. 1951
Hqs. & Hqs. Co., 167th M. P. Bn.	Ahoskie, N. C.	26 Feb. 1951
Co. A, 167th M. P. Bn.	Windsor, N. C.	26 Feb. 1951
121st AAA Operations Detachment	Charlotte, N. C.	14 Dec. 1951
Co. B, 167th M. P. Bn.	Lasker, N. C.	10 April 1952
Btry. D, 725th AAA AW Bn.	Benson, N. C.	14 April 1952

　b. The following Units were reorganized under Public Law 461 as NGUS Units:

Unit	Location	Recognized
Hq. & Hq. Btry., 540th FA Bn., NGUS	High Point, N. C.	2 Nov. 1952
Btry. A, 540th FA Bn., NGUS	High Point, N. C.	3 Nov. 1952
Co. C, 378th Engr. (C) Bn., NGUS	Statesville, N C.	19 Nov. 1952
Hq., Hq. & Svc. Co., 378th Engr. (C) Bn., NGUS	Charlotte, N. C.	20 Nov. 1952
Co. B, 378th Engr. (C) Bn., NGUS	Charlotte, N. C.	20 Nov. 1952
Co. A, 378th Engr. (C) Bn., NGUS	Lincolnton, N.C.	21 Nov. 1952

c. The following Air Units which had been on Active Duty were released and reorganized as follows:

Unit	Location	Recognized
156th Fighter-Intercepter Sqdn.	Charlotte, N. C.	10 July 1952
263rd Comm. Sqdn. Operations	Wadesboro & Badin, N. C.	8 Oct. 1952

4. Construction

During the Calendar Years 1951 and 1952, contracts were entered into for the following projects:

Army National Guard

Project	Location	Cost
Construction of Motor Vehicle storage Building, Masonry Type	Southern Pines, N. C.	$ 28,825.00
Motor Vehicle Storage Building, Masonry Type	Rocky Mount, N. C.	23,250.00
Motor Vehicle Storage Building, Masonry Type	Apex, N. C.	25,780.00
Painting 7MRS Shop Building	Butner, N. C.	4,865.00

Air National Guard

Project	Location	Cost
Extension of NE & SW Run-way	Morris Field, Charlotte, N. C.	$ 811,748.50

All the above projects were financed 100 percent by the Federal Government.

5. Service Contracts

The Federal Government enters into Service Contracts with the Adjutant General's Department, State of North Carolina, for the support of the following installations:

Army National Guard

Location	Activity	Maximun Fed. Got. Support
Butner, N. C.	USP&DO Warehouse & State Maint. Shop	$ 15,000.00
Bluenthenthal Field	AAA Units, Wilmington, N. C.	8,058.00
Raleigh-Durham Airport	Aviation Section, Hq. Co. 30th Division	1,035.00

Air National Guard

Location	Activity	
Morris Field, Charlotte, N. C.	156th Ftr-Intercepter Sqdn.	21,500.00
Badin, N. C.	263rd Comm. Sqdn. Operations	1,500.00
Wadesboro, N. C.	263rd Comm. Sqdn. Operations	1,500.00

These projects are supported on a pro rata basis, the Federal Government bearing 75 per cent of the cost and the State paying 25 per cent of the cost of the operation. The State makes the disbursement for the support of the installations and is reimbursed in the amount of 75 per cent up to the maximum amount for each project as indicated in the above tables.

6. The following facts are of interest and will show the amount of funds expended by the Federal Government in support of the North Carolina National Guard:

Army National Guard

Expenditures of Federal Funds for Fiscal Year Ending 30 June 1951

Construction of Motor Vehicle Storage Buildings	$ 74,855.00
Maintenance and Operation of NCNG Units	85,077.17
Pay of Civilian Personnel	746,467.57
Operation of Other Facilities	27,925.14
(Including Service Contracts which are financed 75 per cent by the Federal Government and 25 per cent by the State)	
Field Training Expenses	748,638.34
Unit Staff Schools	39,047.66
Inactive Duty Training	241,018.97
	$1,963,029.85

Expenditures of Federal Funds for Fiscal year Ending 30 June 1952

Maintenance and Operation of NCNG Units	$ 63,949.83
Pay of Civilian Personnel	851,727.88
Operation of Other Facilities	16,132.57
(Including Service Contracts which are financed 75 per cent by the Federal Government and 25 per cent by the State)	
Field Training Expenses	765,092.39
Unit Staff Schools	32,577.49
Inactive Duty Training	150,569.77
	$1,880,049.93

Air National Guard

Expenditures of Federal Funds for Fiscal Year Ending 30 June 1951

Distribution of Material	$ 6,057.13
Schools and Training	1,451.41
Pay of Civilian Personnel	108,706.99
Maintenance and Operation of ANG Units	17,384.76
Air Combat Maneuvers	38,547.29
	$ 172,147.58

Expenditures of Federal Funds for Fiscal Year Ending 30 June 1952

Construction	$ 823,035.50
Distribution of Material	665.88
Pay of Civilian Personnel	51,893.39
Maintenance and Operation of ANG Units	9,577.96
Air Combat Maneuvers	821.04
Major Repair and Minor Construction	4,191.00
	$ 890,184.77

The above tabulation does not include expenditures for the forty-eight (48) paid Armory Drills.

The following tabulation is made in order to show the amount of detail required to perform the duties incident to the operation of this Office.

Army National Guard

Requisitions forwarded to Depots and higher Headquarters for Supply, Fiscal Year 1951	884
Requisitions forwarded to Depots and higher Headquarters for Supply, Fiscal Year 1952	790
Reports of Survey processed and forwarded to Higher Headquarters, Fiscal Year 1951	138
Reports of Survey processed and fowarded to Higher Headquarters, Fiscal Year 1952	79
Number of Bills of Lading issued, Fiscal Year 1951	208
Number of Bills of Lading issued, Fiscal Year 1952	246
Number of Transportation Requests issued, Fiscal Year 1951	715
Number of Transportation Requests issued, Fiscal Year 1952	852
Number of Certificates of Droppage processed, Fiscal Year 1951	318
Number of Certificates of Droppage processed, Fiscal Year 1952	352
Number of Purchase and Delivery Orders issued, Fiscal Year 1951	834
Number of Purchase and Delivery Orders issued, Fiscal Year 1952	994
Vouchers processed and forwarded to Finance Office, U. S. Army, Atlanta, Georgia, for payment, Fiscal Year 1951	2,111
Vouchers processed and forwarded to Finance Office, U. S. Army, Atlanta, Georgia, for payment, Fiscal Year 1952	2,152
Number of Property Vouchers processed, Fiscal Year 1951	11,388
(Of this number, three hundred and four (304) were Department of the Army, NGB Forms 18 indicating a collection for lost property.)	
Number of Property Vouchers processed, Fiscal Year 1952	10,963
(of this number, five hundred and six (506) were Department of the Army, NGB Forms 18 indicating a collection for lost property.)	

Air National Guard

Number of Property Vouchers processed, Fiscal Year 1951	2,288
Number of Property Vouchers processed, Fiscal Year 1952	912
Requisitions forwarded to Depots, Fiscal Year 1951	531
Requisitions forwarded to Depots, Fiscal Year 1952	424

Practically the whole time during the above two (2) years, the Air National Guard Units were on extended active duty and the number of vouchers and requisitions pertaining to Air Units was greatly reduced on this account.

7. During the Calendar Years 1951 and 1952, the National Guard Bureau inaugurated programs pertaining to equipment which greatly increased the work load of the Office and Warehouse. All World War II vehicles were withdrawn from the National Guard and replaced with new vehicles. Also, certain items of equipment were withdrawn from the National Guard and turned back into Army stocks. Inasmuch as all the vehicles on hand were replaced, all parts pertaining to the old vehicles were turned into Depots. Then before our program of turn in of parts could be completed, it was necessary to receive and issue to all Units new type vehicles and set up a stock of parts pertaining thereto. While this program was in full swing, Warehouse personnel were not able to perform any other duties except to a limited extent.

8. During the period covered by this report, the Department of the Army and the National Guard Bureau determined that the National Guard had quantities of equipment over and above the amount which was actually needed for training. Instructions were received to the effect that Units should turn

in all equipment which was over and above the foreseeable requirements for training. This caused a large quantity of equipment to be returned to the Warehouse. It was packed and turned into Army Depots.

9. Following is a list of personnel occupying key positions or positions as Head of Sections in this Office:

Administrative Assistant	John A. Jones
Chief Clerk	Captain Richard G. York
Field Auditor & Inspector	Lt. Hugh P. Massengill
Field Auditor & Inspector	Maj. Neil J. Pait, Jr.
Field Auditor & Inspector	Maj. James S. Coxe
Transportation Section	Captain Walter C. Lewis
Fiscal Section	Lt. Graydon C. Liles
Purchase and Contract Section	Captain Eugene E. Greene
Property Record Section	Lt. Thomas E. Carter
Supervisor, USP&DO Warehouse	Captain Robert J. Wilkins
Air Section	David L. Graham

10. In accordance with the National Defense Act and the regulations published by the National Guard Bureau, this Office was inspected by the Inspector General, Third Army, as follows:

9-11 April 1951—Inspector General, Major Owen W. Owens
    Rating received "Superior"

17-19 March 1952—Inspector General, Lt. Colonel Russell E. McMurray
    Rating received "Superior"

11. Cooperation on the part of the Adjutant General of this State, Army Instructors, and Advisors, Organization Commanders, and other individual Officers and men has made it possible for this Office to satisfactorily discharge the duties assigned and has made the work a real pleasure. In the operation of this Office for the period covered by this Report, I desire to acknowledge the contribution made and fine assistance rendered by each employee of this Office. Without their untiring work and efforts, the work could not have been done in an acceptable manner.

M. H. AUSTELL
Lt. Colonel, NGB
Acting U. S. Property & Disbursing
Officer, N. C.

1951 FIELD TRAINING REPORTS

August 9, 1951

SUBJECT: Report of Field Training, Selective Service Section, Headquarters & Headquarters Detachment, NC NG, 1-29 July 1951.

TO : The Adjutant General
Raleigh, North Carolina

1. Pursuant to Paragraph 3, GO No. 17, AGD, 18 June 1951, the Report of the Field Training Period, 1-29 July 1951, Selective Service Section, Headquarters & Headquarters Detachment, NC NG, is respectfully submitted herein. Although the General Orders cited provided that this report be submitted by the Commanding Officer, I am, with your consent, submitting the report in view of the fact that I have been assigned responsibility for the training, and the further fact that the period of training was split. The six officers of this section who are not on extended active duty were all present for a two weeks training period, with the exception of Captain Thomas C. Brown, who was excused from one week of such training under the provisions of Paragraph 5, SO 525, AGD, 28 June 1951. The training was conducted in the office of State Headquarters, North Carolina Selective Service System.

2. Believing that the best training would come from actual participation in Selective Service operation the Adjutant General recommended to the National Guard Bureau that the officers of this section be authorized to participate in field training in groups of three, which represented the largest number that could be integrated into the State Headquarters Staff at one time. The recommendation met with the approval of the Director of Selective Service and the National Guard Bureau, and we understand that it was considered with such favor that the idea was suggested for the training of the Selective Service Section in other states and that many adopted it. Splitting the group up presented a few minor administrative disadvantages but in the opinion of the undersigned these in no way were comparable to the advantages of this training method. The officers attending Field Training appeared to have a greater interest in their training and nearly every one of them expressed to the undersigned their individual belief that they had acquired more from this period of Field Training than any other in which they have participated since assignment to the Selective Service Section. From my observation I feel that there is no doubt but what this method of training is the most effective as long as a Selective Service operation is in effect.

3. Since the officers attending Field Training were integrated into the staff of this headquarters no training schedule was prepared, as they were governed by the same hours, regulations and requirements as the staff of this headquarters.

REPORT OF THE ADJUTANT GENERAL 25

4. Attached hereto are copies of the Morning Reports, Selective Service Section, Headquarters & Headquarters Detachment, NC NG, for the period 1-29 July 1951.

                Respectfully,

                THOMAS H. UPTON
                Colonel, FC NGUS
                State Director

cc: Senior Army Instructor
   North Carolina National Guard
   Raleigh, North Carolina

   The Director of Selective Service
   1712 G Street, N. W.
   Washington 25, D. C.

THU:mpt

1951-1952 REPORTS FIELD TRAINING
(Summer Camps)

HEADQUARTERS 252d AAA GROUP
NORTH CAROLINA NATIONAL GUARD
Wilmington, North Carolina

354   21 Aug 51

SUBJECT: Report on Field Training 1951.

TO: The Adjutant General
         State of North Carolina
         Justice Building
         Raleigh, North Carolina

1. In compliance with par. 5, General Order No. 16, Adjutant General's Department, State of North Carolina, Raleigh, North Carolina, dated 14 June 1951, submitted herewith a report on the field training of this headquarters 8-22 July 1951 inclusive.

2. PERSONNEL—The 252d AAA Group consisted of approximately 320 officers and enlisted men. This number was made up of both assigned and attached units of the North Carolina National Guard as follows:

    A. Assigned—Hq Hq Btry 252d AAA Gp..........................Wilmington, N. C.
                    Hq Hq Btry 725th AAA AW Bn.......................Whiteville, N. C.
                    Btry A, 725th AAA AW Bn..............................Shallotte, N. C.
                    Btry B, 725th AAA AW Bn............................Fair Bluff, N. C.
                    Btry C, 725th AAA AW Bn............................Bladenboro, N. C.

    B. Attached—94th Army Band..Raleigh, N. C.
                    217th RCAT Det..Raleigh, N. C.
                    3624th Ord Med Maint Co............................Butner, N. C.
                    (1 Officer)

    C. The 123rd SRMU assigned to this command did not attend camp as all enlisted personnel were in school. The Commanding Officer was attached to Hq Hq Btry, 252d AAA Group for field training.

3. MOVEMENT—The movement by units of the 252d AAA Group to Camp Stewart, Georgia for the field training period was executed in three phases: Advance Party by Motor, Main Body by Rail, and Main Body by Motor.

    a. Advance party from Wilmington, N. C., Hq Hq Btry 252d AAA Group, left home station at 0800 hours, 5 July 1951, and proceeded to a prearranged bivouac area approximately one-half mile south of Green Pond, South Carolina. The advance party from Bladenboro, N. C., Btry C, 725th AAA AW Bn, left home station at 0615 hours, 5 July 1951, and traveled to Whiteville, N. C., clearing Whiteville with Hq Hq Btry, 725th AAA AW Bn, at 0700 hours. The advance party from Shallotte, N. C., Btry A, 725th AAA AW Bn, cleared at 0700 hours and proceeded to Georgetown, South Carolina, where it joined serials from Whiteville and Bladenboro, N. C. traveling in two columns to the bivouac area near Green Pond, South Carolina. Advance party from Fair Bluff, N. C., Btry B, 725th AAA AW Bn, left its home station at 0700 hours the same day and joined the remainder of the group at the bivouac area, Green Pond, South Carolina. The assembled advance unit departed from the bivouac area at 0700 hours, 6 July 1951, and arrived at Camp Stewart, Georgia 1030 hours, 6 July 1951.

b. The main body by motor was conducted in two serials; the 725th AAA AW Bn in one serial proceeding under their own orders departed home stations 7 July 1951, and arrived at Camp Stewart, Ga. 1115 hours 8 July 1951. The other serial was composed of Hq Hq Btry, 252d AAA Gp which left its home station 0800 hours, 7 July 1951, and bivouaced for the night 3.1 miles south of RJ 303 SC Hiway 32 at Myrtle Grove Plantation. This unit arrived at Camp Stewart, Georgia, 1030 hours, 8 July 1951.

c. The main body by rail from Wilmington, N. C. left by Atlantic Coast Line train Extra at 0600 hours, 8 July 1951, and was joined in Whiteville, N. C. by main body by rail from that station. Main body by rail from Bladenboro and Shallotte departed from their home stations by commercial bus in time to meet ACL train Extra, joining the Whiteville and Wilmington units in Whiteville. This serial proceeded to Fair Bluff, N. C. picking up Btry C, 725th AAA AW Bn, and arrived at Camp Stewart, Georgia at 1645 hours, 8 July 1951.

d. All units composing the train movement ate breakfast at their home stations and were furnished box lunches for the midday meal which were consumed enroute.

e. Motor units returned to their home stations by the same means stated above in reverse order, leaving Camp Stewart in time to arrive home station 22 July 1951. The movement by rail was scheduled to leave Camp Stewart, Ga. at 0600 hours, 22 July 1951, and to arrive at home station 1640 hours, 22 July 1951; however, these orders were amended, and units left Camp Stewart 2100 hours 21 July 1951, arriving home stations by 0740 hours, 22 July 1951. Rear detachments of all units arrived home stations 23 July 1951.

f. Usual convoy discipline was observed on the motor movements with rest and meal stops at the proper intervals. There were no accidents or motor troubles during the motor movement nor any accidents during the rail movement. The entire move both to and from Camp Stewart, Ga. was very orderly and executed in the best possible military manner.

4. CAMP SITE—The camp site was made up of a tent area for living quarters with buildings for all headquarters, supply rooms, vehicle maintenance shops, and mess halls. All personnel, both commissioned and enlisted, occupied squad tents. These tents had concrete floors, electric lights, and were screened. Water did not drain too readily from the area after rain storms. All personnel had mosquito bars but they were not used as there were no mosquitoes or insects. All post facilities were operating and were only a short distance away.

5. SUPPLIES—a. The G-4 section at Camp Stewart, Georgia, was most cooperative in assisting to secure supplies; however, the administrative work

involved before items could be issued by the various offices caused considerable delay. The system which they used was very good for permanent units but since this organization was to be there only a short period, it is felt that special consideration should have been given requests for supplies and equipment. In one instance the Group Supply Officer was directed to four warehouses before he arrived at the place where the items were stored, consuming the greater part of the morning. Sometimes it would be necessary to wait for an hour or more at an office in an effort to have an Issue Slip approved. A number of items which were in short supply were not available on a loan basis for training. These included radios and motor transportation. The U. S. Prop. & Disb. Officer for North Carolina had a representative at the field training site. He signed directly to the issuing office for items requested and in turn secured signatures of the persons to whom they were delivered. He procured ammunition and gasoline and directed the turn-in of property at the end of the encampment. Cots, mattresses, and mattress covers were drawn from and returned to supply rooms within the area which saved considerable time as well as wear and tear had it been necessary to return them to various warehouses.

b. Four mess halls were operated this year, three enlisted and one officers' mess. Selected mess personnel attended a pre-camp mess school for three days prior to the arrival of the main body of troops. This school was conducted by experienced instructors from Third Army and proved to be very helpful. Officers ate at the unit officers' mess, and payment was made by payroll deduction in the majority of cases. Civilian personnel were hired to assist in this mess, and each officer contributed toward this cost and also the cost of supplementary rations.

c. The quantity of food as set forth under the Master Menu, as amended, did not appear to be as large as that for the previous summer encampment. A remark was made by one of the personnel at the ration breakdown to the effect that he did not see the necessity for a special menu as the menu for the troops on active duty was better. Each mess hall at sometime during the encampment ran short on some items, especially bread and potatoes. Some of the shortages were possibly due to lack of supervision and improper preparation, but as a general rule there were no seconds available. The appetites of the men did not begin to taper off until about the middle of the second week. There were items in the menu which ran the cost up considerably and for which a suitable substitution could have been made at a lower cost. The men want substantial meals rather than fancy food to which they are not accustomed at home. Items such as cantaloupe, frozen asparagus, frozen garden peas, frozen broccoli, fresh plums and fresh peaches were not popular. Other excessive items were dry cereal, coffee, jam, jelly, and onions. The following items should be increased: sugar, flour, potatoes, bread, and tea.

6. TRAINING—a. Throughout the two week period, training was carried out according to the approved schedule, issued prior to camp, with very few changes. A great interest in all phases of training was shown by the men. Schools were conducted for communications men, radio operators, battery clerks, first sergeants, and intelligence personnel. The 725th AAA AW Bn did an excellent job of firing with their crew-served weapons which consisted

of 40 mm's and M55's. A great number of hits were scored on the aerial towed sleeve targets and several OQ-19 radio controlled planes were shot down.

b. Small arms firing was conducted in order that all men who had not qualified in small arms or who had joined the National Guard since the week-end firing could be qualified. This firing was conducted on "B" Range by this headquarters.

c. On Tuesday, 17 July 1951, Hq and Hq Btry, 252d AAA Gp, and the 725th AAA AW Bn moved into the field for a three day field problem. The 725th AAA AW Bn set up the AAA defense of a bridge using all the field equipment issued to them. Since units did not have 100% strength or full T/O equipment, some of the gun positions had to be simulated. Practice strafing and low level bombing attacks by an Air Force A-26 plane were flown. An attack by an aggressor force to test the local ground defense of the positions was called off because of rain. The field problem was terminated at 2200 hours 19 July 1951 because of a severe rain storm that flooded most of the gun positions. However, the storm offered an excellent opportunity to train all personnel in that the move back into camp was made under the most adverse weather conditions. Morale in the field even during the rain storm was very high and the proficiency of all men was demonstrated.

d. The 94th Army Band, NC NG, assisted materially in gaining the maximum benefit from the training scheduled. They played at all formations, reveille, retreat, dismounted drill, practice parades, and at all ceremonies.

e. A detachment from the 3624th Ord Med Maint. Company functioned most efficiently during the field training period. This detachment performed such maintenance as was beyond the capabilities of organizational personnel. The burden of the post ordnance personnel was greatly relieved by their presence. The willing, cooperative, and efficient manner exhibited by this unit was most gratifying.

f. The 217th RCAT Detachment, NC NG, assisted the Third Army AAA Training Center RCAT Detachment by flying all radio controlled targets for the 725th AAA AW Bn during the firing. They relieved the burden of the Post RCAT Detachment greatly, and gained much experience flying and maintaining target planes.

g. This command offered a number of trophies to be awarded at the end of the encampment. A group of officers, whose identity remained unknown, judged the events. Units were judged during the full two week period and awards given for events. Award winners were as follows:

Award	*Winning Unit*
Highest Percentage of Attendance at Camp	Hq Btry, 252d AAA Gp
Military Efficiency	Btry C, 725th AAA AW Bn
Military Appearance	94th Army Band
Best Mess Hall	Duplicate awards were made to Hq Btry and Btry A, 725th AAA AW Bn, who operated a joint mess.

These awards were presented at the Post Theatre on 21 July 1951 by the Group Commander. At this assembly the 94th Army Band was awarded the

Eisenhower Trophy for the third consecutive time for excellence during the past year.

h. Post personnel and the AAA instruction teams from Fort Bliss, Texas, were very helpful, cooperative, and implemented the successful manner in which the training was carried out.

i. Training for the fourth field training period was well coordinated, and at all times was conducted in an effort to accomplish all possible training that could not be conducted during the armory training periods with any degree of practicability.

7. INSPECTIONS—During the field training period training and administration inspections were conducted by several higher headquarters in an effort to evaluate the state of training, efficiency, and status of admniistration and supply of all units in this command. Inspectors appeared to be generally interested in the units and offered many worthwhile suggestions. The following representatives of the headquarters indicated below inspected:

Headquarters   *Inspector*

DEPARTMENTS OF THE ARMY AND THE AIR FORCE

    Army Field Forces............................Lt. Col. Gay E. Miller
                                                    G-3

    National Guard Bureau....................Lt. Col. James E. Barbor
                                                    Training
                                                    Lt. Col. Clifford L. Smires
                                                    Logistics

    Third Army ....Maj. Gen. Biederlinden
                                                    Deputy Commander
                                                    Lt. Col. Paul A. Eckstein
                                                    Actg. Ass't Insp. Gen.
                                                    Maj. Donald Simon
                                                    Actg. Ass't Insp. Gen.

    Senior Instructor, NC NG...............Col. Lee Bizzell
                                                    Senior Inst.

NORTH CAROLINA NATIONAL GUARD

    U. S. Prop. & Disb. Offr. for N. C....Lt. Col. Michael H. Austell
                                                    Actg. USP & DO for N. C.

    IV Corps Artillery............................Lt. Col. Ivan G. Walz
                                                    Army Artillery Inst.
                                                    Capt. Charles D. Isom
                                                    Adm. Ass't.

8. COMMENDATIONS—Brigadier General Clare H. Armstrong, Commanding General, and his entire staff at Camp Stewart, Georgia, for their helpful, courteous efficient assistance in making the camp a success.

Colonel Frederick L. Van Atta, Army Artillery Advisor, Major Frank Shelton, Army Artillery Intructor, and their assistants, Master Sergeant Alvin A.

Bischoff, and Sergeant First Class John H. Highsmith, for their splendid attitude and effective instruction in all fields.

9. RECOMMENDATIONS—

1. The representative of the U. S. Prop. & Disb. Officer for North Carolina should arrive at the field training site at least one (1) day prior to the arrival of the advance detachment so that PC & S property will all be inventoried and signed to the State thus minimizing the delay in the issue of this property to using units. Recommend that this representative, upon arrival, report immediately to Post Headquarters, a custom long followed in the military service. His failure to follow this procedure this year resulted in several changes in plans.

2. Recommend that the 217th RCAT Detachment, NC NG, and the 94th Army Band, NC NG, be attached to this headquarters for the next field training period.

3. Recommend that a detachment from the 3624th Ord Med Maint Company be attached to this headquarters to perform maintenance beyond the capabilities of organizational shops.

4. Suggest that steps be taken to overcome the problem of feeding troops enroute to the field training site. Railroad station restaurants are unsanitary and overcrowded and in the past have not been able to furnish satisfactory meals. Recommend that a diner be attached to the troop train.

5. Recommend that the movement to the field training site begin on Saturday and Pullmans be provided for all personnel. The movement as scheduled, leaving Wilmington, N. C. at 0600 hours, required all personnel to leave home in the middle of the night and on the return trip would not allow time during daylight hours for the unloading and unpacking of property and baggage.

6. Recommend that AAA instruction teams be made available for future encampments.

7. Request that an ambulance and adequate medical support be available.

8. Request that the tent area be assigned to this organization well in advance of the field training period, and a minimum number of adjustments made.

9. The need for additional vehicles will continue until all units have been issued additional trucks as authorized by the T/O & E. Recommend that vehicles be made available on a loan basis for future camps.

10. Recommend that the monetary value of rations drawn be forwarded to this headquarters regularly to insure against ovedrawing the ration account.

11. Recommend that special consideration be accorded supply requests submitted during the field training period because of the limited time involved.

12. Recommend that the ration of bread and potatoes be increased and frozen vegetables decreased.

13. Recommend that the jam, jelly, and coffee ration components be reduced.

14. Recommend that the Pre-Camp Mess Training Courses be continued prior to future camps.

15. Request that this headquarters be advised of the attachment of reservists in advance of field training.

KENNETH M. CORBETT
Colonel, Arty.
Commanding

Copies Furnished:

    USP&DO for NC
    Senior Inst., NC NG
    Army Arty Inst., IV Corps
    Army Arty Advisor, 252d AAA Gp
    Army Arty Inst., 725th AAA AW Bn

STATE OF NORTH CAROLINA
Office of the
STATE DIRECTOR OF SELECTIVE SERVICE
RALEIGH

4 August 1952

In Reply Refer To: 8.4-1g

SUBJECT: Report of Field Training
                Selective Service Section
                Headquarters & Headquarters Detachment, NCNG

TO: The Adjutant General
             Raleigh
             North Carolina

1. Pursuant to paragraph 3, General Orders No. 12, AGD, Raleigh, North Carolina, 25 June 1952, we submit herewith report on field training, Selective Service Section, Headquarters and Headquarters Detachment, NCNG, for the period 6 July 1952 to 3 August 1952.

2. The section, pursuant to recommendations based on previous experience, trained in two separate groups of three each. We are still of the opinion that it is more beneficial to break the unit into small groups in order that they can be given personal training in the State Headquarters. The State Headquarters cannot adequately handle the training of a larger group without some loss of effectiveness. The training this year was devoted to three divisions of State Headquarters which are considered to be somewhat specialized; i.e., Procurement and Fiscal, Personnel, and Manpower. The trainees were allotted three days in each division and one day was used in a general critique to permit the trainees to compare notes and to question more closely the chiefs of the divisions when they found any discrepancies to exist between their own personal notes or understanding of the operations.

3. From the comments of the trainees, we believe that the training was highly successful and that each trainee now has a greater conception of the function and relation of those divisions which are mainly administrative

and which support the main function of the State Headquarters in coordinating and guiding the activities of local boards. The experience of this training period continues to bear out the thought that smaller groups can receive more effective training and we definitely recommend that this thought be followed in future training periods. We also feel that the most adequate training for the Selective Service Section is to be obtained at the State Headquarters, since these officers are being trained for assignment in such Headquarters in event of an emergency.

4. Inclosed is the original copy of Morning Report. DA AGO Form 1, for the period 6 July 1952 to 3 August 1952.

THOMAS H. UPTON
Colonel, FC
State Director

Incls

1951 EXECUTIVE ORDERS

STATE OF NORTH CAROLINA
GOVERNOR'S OFFICE
RALEIGH

EXECUTIVE ORDER   1 August 1951
No.   8

Announcement is made of the appointment of Lieutenant Colonel THOMAS B. LONGEST, O 328 125, AGC, NC NG, as Acting Adjutant General, State of North Carolina, effective 1 August 1951, vice Major General J. VAN B. METTS, O 103 920, retired.

W. KERR SCOTT
Governor and Commander-in-Chief

(Seal)

STATE OF NORTH CAROLINA
GOVERNOR'S OFFICE
RALEIGH

EXECUTIVE ORDER   1 October 1951
No.   9

The appointment of JOHN HALL MANNING, O 207 814, as the Adjutant General of North Carolina with the rank of Major General is announced, effective 1 October 1951.

W. KERR SCOTT
Governor and Commander-in-Chief

(Seal)

1951 GENERAL ORDERS

STATE OF NORTH CAROLINA
ADJUTANT GENERAL'S DEPARTMENT
RALEIGH

GENERAL ORDERS 9 August 1951
No. 24

So much of Par. 2a, General Orders No. 22, this Department, dated 26 July 1951, pertaining to Train Commanders for troop trains moving to Fort McClellan, Alabama for Summer Encampment period as reads, "Major James M. Hayes, Jr., 0-946818," is AMENDED to read, "Captain John B. Wolfe, 0-1553016."

By Order of the Governor:

THOMAS B. LONGEST
The Acting Adjutant General

OFFICIAL
THOMAS B. LONGEST
Lt. Col., NCNG
The Acting Adjutant General

STATE OF NORTH CAROLINA
ADJUTANT GENERAL'S DEPARTMENT
RALEIGH

GENERAL ORDERS 5 September 1951
No. 25

1. Pursuant to Sec. 93, National Defense Act, as amended, and the provisions of Sec. II, National Guard Regulations 48, 4 October 1946, Annual Armory Inspections of the following North Carolina National Guard units will be conducted by officers of the Regular Army detailed by the Commanding General of the Third Army at the places and on the dates indicated:

Unit	Location	Date	Inspector
Hq. Hq. Btry., 725th AAA AW Bn.	Whiteville	8 Oct. 51	Lt. Col. H. R. Tuebner
Btry. B, 725th AAA AW Bn.	Fair Bluff	9 Oct. 51	Lt. Col. H. R. Tuebner
Btry. B, 130th AAA AW Bn.	St. Pauls	10 Oct. 51	Lt. Col. H. R. Tuebner
Btry. C, 725th AAA AW Bn.	Bladenboro	11 Oct. 51	Lt. Col. H. R. Tuebner
Co. I, 119th Inf.	Wilmington	12 Oct. 51	Lt. Col. H. R. Tuebner
Btry. A, 725th AAA AW Bn.	Shallotte	15 Oct. 51	Lt. Col. H. R. Tuebner
Hq. Hq. Co., 167th MP Bn.	Ahoskie	15 Oct. 51	Lt. Col. R. E. McMurray
123d SRMU (Type C)	Wilmington	16 Oct. 51	Lt. Col. H. R. Tubener
Hq. Hq. Btry., 252nd AAA Gp.	Wilmington	16 Oct. 51	Lt. Col. H. R. Tuebner
Hv. Mtr. Co., 119th Inf.	Edenton	16 Oct. 51	Lt. Col. R. E. McMurray
Svc. Co., 119th Inf.	Elizabeth City	17 Oct. 51	Lt. Col. R. E. McMurray
Co. A, 167th MP Bn.	Windsor	18 Oct. 51	Lt. Col. R. E. McMurray
Co. F, 119th Inf.	Tarboro	19 Oct. 51	Lt. Col. R. E. McMurray

Unit	Location	Date	Inspector
Hq. 30th Inf. Div. (In Part)	Raleigh	22 Oct. 51	Col. J. D. Salmon
Hq. Hq. Btry., 112th FA Bn.	Lenoir	22 Oct. 51	Lt. Col. H. R. Tuebner
Co. H, 119th Inf.	Scotland Neck	22 Oct. 51	Lt. Col. R. E. McMurray
Co. A, 119th Inf.	Oxford	22 Oct. 51	Lt. Col. E. P. Curtin
217th RCAT Det.	Raleigh	23 Oct. 51	Col J. D. Salmon
Hq. Hq. Det. NCNG	Raleigh	23 Oct. 51	Col. J. D. Salmon
Svc. Btry., 112th FA Bn.	Lenoir	23 Oct. 51	Lt. Col. H. R. Tuebner
Co. E, 119th Inf.	Roanoke Rpds	23 Oct. 51	Lt. Col. R. E. McMurray
Co. C, 119th Inf.	Henderson	23 Oct. 51	Lt. Col. E. P. Curtin
Btry. C, 113th FA Bn.	Roxboro	24 Oct. 51	Col. J. D. Salmon
Btry. C, 112th FA Bn.	N. Wilkesboro	24 Oct. 51	Lt. Col. H. R. Tuebner
Co. B, 119th Inf.	Warrenton	24 Oct. 51	Lt. Col. E. P. Curtin
Hq. Hq. Btry., 30th Div. Arty (In Part)	Louisburg	25 Oct. 51	Col. J. D. Salmon
Hq. Hq. Btry., 113th FA Bn.	Louisburg	25 Oct. 51	Col. J. D. Salmon
Co. A, 120th Inf.	Burlington	25 Oct. 51	Lt. Col. E. P. Curtin
Svc. Btry., 113th FA Bn.	Youngsville	26 Oct. 51	Col. J. D. Salmon
Hv. Mtr. Co., 120th Inf.	Leaksville	26 Oct. 51	Lt. Col. E. P. Curtin
Btry A 113th FA Bn	Zebulon	29 Oct. 51	Lt. Col. J. D. Salmon
Hq. Hq. Co., 1st Bn, 120th Inf.	Mt. Airy	29 Oct. 51	Lt. Col. E. P. Curtin
94th Army Band	Raleigh	30 Oct. 51	Col. J. D. Salmon
Hq. Hq. Co., 120th Inf.	Reidsville	30 Oct. 51	Lt. Col. E. P. Curtin

2. Armory Inspections will be made in two (2) parts: An administrative inspection of armory facilities, property, official records, and general administration. The organization commander, first sergeant, caretaker, supply sergeant and administrative assistant will be present at the armory at the time designated for the administrative inspection. There will also be an inspection of the state of training of all personnel of the organization and the adequacy of equipment. The time devoted to the training inspection should not exceed the time required in a normal armory drill period. The hours of these two parts of the inspection will be set by arrangement between the unit commander and the inspecting officer.

3. All property, arms, clothing and equipment will be thoroughly cleaned and put in good condition. Property in supply rooms and individual lockers will be neatly and carefully arranged, in order that the inspecting officer may check their condition without a loss of time.

4. Attendance at inspection is compulsory. A report of all absentees from inspection by reason of unavoidable causes, such as sickness, etc., will be rendered to the inspection officer. Absentees without leave of absence will be dealt with in accordance with the law. Officers and enlisted men temporarily absent from their home stations on the date of inspection of their organization may be attached for inspection to any other organization, provided the necessary arrangements are made with the Adjutant General by the immediate commanding officers and notice given the inspector to whom they are to report.

5. The inspection will be formal. The unit commanders will review carefully Sec. II, NGR-48; SR 20-10-8, 21 July 1949, as amended, and present the unit for inspection according to the directives contained therein.

6. The expense enjoined is necessary in the military service.

By Order of the Governor:

THOMAS B. LONGEST
Acting The Adjutant General

OFFICIAL

THOMAS B. LONGEST
Lt. Col., NCNG
Acting The Adjutant General

STATE OF NORTH CAROLINA
ADJUTANT GENERAL'S DEPARTMENT
RALEIGH

GENERAL ORDERS
No. 26
6 September 1951

1. Pursuant to receipt of evidence of enlistment in the U. S. Navy, 17 January 1923, so much of General Orders #2, this headquarters, dated 18 February 1923 pertaining to discharge of Pvt. Webster E. Myers is AMENDED to read "PAC par 348(2c), NGR, 1922, Pvt. Webster E. Myers, Co. F, 120th Inf., NCNG, station Charlotte, N. C. is hereby discharged from the service for purpose of enlisting in the United States Navy, effective 16 January 1923".

By Order of the Governor:

THOMAS B. LONGEST
Acting The Adjutant General

(Seal)

STATE OF NORTH CAROLINA
ADJUTANT GENERAL'S DEPARTMENT
RALEIGH

GENERAL ORDERS
No. 27
25 September 1951

So much of Par. 1, G. O. No. 25, this department, dtd 5 September 1951, pertaining to dates for Annual Armory Inspections of the following units NCNG is RESCINDED and the following substituted therefor:

Co E 119th Inf	16 Oct 51
Btry A 113th FA Bn	22 Oct 51
94th Army Band	23 Oct 51
Hv Mtr Co 119th Inf	23 Oct 51
217th RCAT Det	29 Oct 51
Hq Hq Det NCNG	29 Oct 51
Hq 30th Inf Div (In Part)	30 Oct 51

By Order of the Governor:

THOMAS B. LONGEST
Acting The Adjutant General

OFFICIAL

THOMAS B. LONGEST
Lt. Col., NCNG
Acting The Adjutant General

STATE OF NORTH CAROLINA
ADJUTANT GENERAL'S DEPARTMENT
RALEIGH

GENERAL ORDERS
No. 28   1 October 1951

Colonel Claude T. Bowers, O-183291 GSC, Chief of Staff, 30th Infantry Division (In Part), NC NG, is designated as Commanding Officer of the 30th Infantry Division (In Part), NC NG, in addition to his other duties, effective this date.

By Order of the Governor:

OFFICIAL: JOHN H. MANNING
JOHN H. MANNING   *Major General*
Major General   *The Adjutant General*
The Adjutant General

STATE OF NORTH CAROLINA
ADJUTANT GENERAL'S DEPARTMENT
RALEIGH

GENERAL ORDERS
No. 29   3 October 1951

1. Pursuant to Sec. 93, National Defense Act, as amended, and the provisions of Sec. II, National Guard Regulations 48, 4 October 1946, Annual Armory Inspections of the following North Carolina National Guard units will be conducted by officers of the Regular Army detailed by the Commanding General of the Third Army at the places and on the dates indicated:

Unit	Location	Date	Inspector
Btry. B, 112th FA Bn	Spindale	5 Nov. 51	Col. J. D. Salmon
Btry. C, 130th AAA AW Bn.	Sanford	5 Nov. 51	Lt. Col. R. E. McMurray
Co. B, 120th Inf.	Winston-Salem	5 Nov. 51	Lt. Col. E. P. Curtin
Btry. A, 112th FA Bn.	Forest City	6 Nov. 51	Col. J. D. Salmon
Btry. B, 113th FA Bn.	Dunn	6 Nov. 51	Lt. Col. R. E. McMurray
Co. D, 120th Inf.	Winston-Salem	6 Nov. 51	Lt. Col. E. P. Curtin
Hq. Hq. Co., 3d Bn., 120th Inf.	Kings Mtn	7 Nov. 51	Col. J. D. Salmon
Co. K, 119th Inf.	Fayetteville	7 Nov. 51	Lt. Col. R. E. McMurray
Med. Co., 120th Inf.	Mocksville	7 Nov. 51	Lt. Col. E. P. Curtin
Hq. Hq. Btry., IV Corps Arty.	Charlotte	8 Nov. 51	Col. J. D. Salmon
Mdm. Tk. Co., 119th Inf.	Parkton	8 Nov. 51	Lt. Col. R. E. McMurray
Co. C, 120th Inf.	Lexington	8 Nov. 51	Lt. Col. E. P. Curtin
Med. Det., 505th FA Bn.	Greensboro	9 Nov. 51	Col. J. D. Salmon
Hq. Hq. Btry., 505th FA Bn.	Greensboro	9 Nov. 51	Col. J. D. Salmon
Btry. D, 130th AAA AW Bn.	Southern Pines	9 Nov. 51	Lt. Col. R. E. McMurray
Co. G, 120th Inf.	Salisbury	9 Nov. 51	Lt. Col. E. P. Curtin
Svc. Btry., 505th FA Bn.	Greensboro	12 Nov. 51	Col. J. D. Salmon
Hq. Hq. Co. 1st Bn., 119th Inf.	Durham	12 Nov. 51	Lt. Col. R. E. McMurray
Co. F, 120th Inf.	Albemarle	12 Nov. 51	Lt. Col. E. P. Curtin

REPORT OF THE ADJUTANT GENERAL 29

Unit	Location	Date	Inspector
Btry. C, 505th FA Bn.	Greensboro	13 Nov. 51	Col. J. D. Salmon
Hq. Hq. Co., 119th Inf.	Durham	13 Nov. 51	Lt. Col. R. E. McMurray
Hq. Hq. Co., 2d Bn., 120th Inf.	Asheboro	13 Nov. 51	Lt. Col. E. P. Curtin
Btry. A, 505th FA Bn.	Greensboro	14 Nov. 51	Col. J. D. Salmon
Co. D, 119th Inf.	Durham	14 Nov. 51	Lt. Col. R. E. McMurray
Co. E, 120th Inf.	Concord	14 Nov. 51	Lt. Col. E. P. Curtin
Hq. Hq. Btry., 252d FA Gp.	Greensboro	15 Nov. 51	Col. J. D. Salmon
3624th Ord M Co.	Durham	15 Nov. 51	Lt. Col. R. E. McMurray
Co. L, 120th Inf.	Morganton	15 Nov. 51	Lt. Col. E. P. Curtin
Btry. B, 505th FA Bn.	Greensboro	16 Nov. 51	Col. J. D. Salmon
Med. Det., 30th Inf. Div.	Apex	16 Nov. 51	Lt. Col. R. E. McMurray
Hq. Co., 30th Inf. Div.	Apex	16 Nov. 51	Lt. Col. R. E. McMurray
Co. H, 120th Inf.	Hickory	16 Nov. 51	Lt. Col. E. P. Curtin
Btry. A, 130th AAA AW Bn.	Raeford	26 Nov. 51	Col. J. D. Salmon
Co. M, 130th Inf.	Shelby	26 Nov. 51	Maj. E. W. Buchanan
Hq. Hq. Btry., 130th AAA AW Bn.	Red Springs	27 Nov. 51	Col. J. D. Salmon
Co. I, 120th Inf.	Newton	27 Nov. 51	Maj. E. W. Buchanan
Co. K, 120th Inf.	Gastonia	28 Nov. 51	Maj. E. W. Buchanan

2. Armory Inspections will be made in two (2) parts: An administrative inspection of armory facilities, property, official records, and general administration. The organization commander, first sergeant, caretaker, supply sergeant and administrative assistant will be present at the armory at the time designated for the administrative inspection. There will also be an inspection of the state of training of all personnel of the organization and the adequacy of equipment. The time devoted to the training inspection should not exceed the time required in a normal armory drill period. The hours of these two parts of the inspection will be set by arrangement between the unit commander and the inspecting officer.

3. All property, arms, clothing and equipment will be thoroughly cleaned and put in good condition. Property in supply rooms and individual lockers will be neatly and carefully arranged, in order that the inspecting officer may check their condition without a loss of time.

4. Attendance at inspection is compulsory. A report of all absentees from inspection by reason of unavoidable causes, such as sickness, etc., will be rendered to the inspection officer. Absentees without leave of absence will be dealt with in accordance with the law. Officers and enlisted men temporarily absent from their home stations on the date of inspection of their organization may be attached for inspection to any other organization, provided the necessary arrangements are made with the Adjutant General by the immediate commanding officers and notice given the inspector to whom they are to report.

5. The inspection will be formal. The unit commanders will review carefully Sec. II, NGR-48; SR 20-10-8, 21 July 1949, as amended, and present the unit for inspection according to the directives contained therein.

6. The expense enjoined is necessary in the military service.

By Order of the Governor:

OFFICIAL:
JOHN H. MANNING
Major General
The Adjutant General

JOHN H. MANNING
Major General
The Adjutant General

STATE OF NORTH CAROLINA
ADJUTANT GENERAL'S DEPARTMENT
RALEIGH

GENERAL ORDERS
No.   30   3 October 1951

1. PAC Letter, NGB, NG-AROTO—Gen, Subject: Reorganization of the Signal Company, National Guard Infantry Division, dated 27 September 1951, the 30th Signal Company, North Carolina National Guard, is hereby reorganized in accordance with T/O&E and change indicated below, effective 1 November 1951. Maximum authorized strength for officers and warrant officers is listed in Column 7 and enlisted strength in Column 8 of appropriate T/O&E or change thereto.

Unit & Designation	T/O&E & Date		Applicable Changes	
	No.	Date	No.	Date
30th Signal Company, 30th Infantry Division	11-7N	3 May 48	3	14 Apr. 51

2. The provisions of NGB Circular No. 22, dated 24 September 1948, and NGB Circular No. 4, dated 1 March 1949, apply to this reorganization.

3. Although total enlisted strength will not exceed that authorized in Column 8 of appropriate T/O&E the number of grades for each MOS shown in Columns 16 through 21 inclusive, Section II (Organization) of the table is authorized. Promotions to higher grades E-7, E-6 and E-5 are hereby authorized provided individuals are fully qualified and meet the requirements outlined in the three year training program. As a minimum requirement, grade positions listed in Column 22 ((Enlisted Cadre) are prescribed for the initial selection for grades E-7, E-6 and E-5.

4. Letter, NG-AROTO, 23 February 1951, Subject: Department of the Army Changes to Section III (Equipment) of T/O&E, applies insofar as Section III (Equipment) of the Tables is concerned.

By Order of the Governor:

OFFICIAL:
JOHN H. MANNING
Major General
The Adjutant General

JOHN H. MANNING
Major General
The Adjutant General

REPORT OF THE ADJUTANT GENERAL

STATE OF NORTH CAROLINA
ADJUTANT GENERAL'S DEPARTMENT
RALEIGH

GENERAL ORDERS 11 October 1951
No.   31

PAC NGR-20 11 Dec 47 MAJOR GENERAL JOHN HALL MANNING O 207 814 Inf NCNG is rel of further asg as CG (SSN 0002) Hq 30th Inf Div (In Part) NCNG sta Raleigh NC and asg Hq Hq Det NCNG sta Raleigh NC EDCSA 1 Oct 51 vice Major General J. Van B. Metts 0 103 920 retired.

By Order of the Governor:

OFFICIAL:
DAVID W. DONOVAN
Military Personnel Officer
The Adjutant General's Dept.

JOHN H. MANNING
Major General
The Adjutant General

STATE OF NORTH CAROLINA
ADJUTANT GENERAL'S DEPARTMENT
RALEIGH

GENERAL ORDERS 1 November 1951
No.   32

1. PAC Ltr, NGB, NG-AFOTP, Subject: "Authorization for Headquarters, North Carolina Air National Guard," dated 31 Aug 1951, the Headquarters, North Carolina Air National Guard is organized effective this date under Section II B, T/D ANG 1-100, dated 1 Sept 1951.

2. Personnel and equipment now assigned to the Air Section, State Hq & Hq Detachment, NCNG, will be transferred to Hq, NC ANG effective this date.

3. Temporary additional military spaces authorized the Air Section, Hq & Hq Detachment, NCNG, as Air Base Flight "B" is authorized the Hq, NC ANG as Air Base Flight "B", with no change in authorization or mission.

4. In view of organization referred to above, the Air Section, State Hq & Hq Detachment, NCNG, is inactivated this date.

By Order of the Governor:

OFFICIAL:
THOMAS B. LONGEST
Military Operations Officer
Adjutant General's Department

JOHN H. MANNING
Major General
The Adjutant General

REPORT OF THE ADJUTANT GENERAL

STATE OF NORTH CAROLINA
ADJUTANT GENERAL'S DEPARTMENT
RALEIGH

GENERAL ORDERS 5 November 1951
No. 33

PAC Amendment No. 2 to TA No. 31-B, NGB, dated 30 October 1951, so much of G. O. No. 22, this Department, dated 26 July 1951, as authorizes 16 days Field Training time for elements of Hq Hq Btry, IV Corps Arty, NCNG, is AMENDED to authorize 18 days for one (1) officer traveling by Government motor from home station, Midway Park, North Carolina, to Fort McClellan, Alabama.

By Order of the Governor:

OFFICIAL:
THOMAS B. LONGEST
Military Operations Officer
Adjutant General's Department

JOHN H. MANNING
Major General
The Adjutant General

STATE OF NORTH CAROLINA
ADJUTANT GENERAL'S DEPARTMENT
RALEIGH

GENERAL ORDERS 7 November 1951
No. 34

Reorganization of Hq Hq Detch NCNG

PAC Ltr, NGB, NG-AROTO 325.4—N. C., Subject: Table of Organization, State Headquarters and Headquarters Detachment, dated 29 October 1951, the Headquarters and Headquarters Detachment, North Carolina National Guard, is reorganized in accordance with the following Table of Organization, effective 1 November 1951:

Line	Grade	National Guard	Augmentation For Selective Service	Total
1	Maj. Gen.			
2	Brig. Gen.	1		1
3	Colonel	2	2	4
4	Lt. Colonel	5	4	9
5	Major	2	7	9
6	Captain	3	2	5
7	1st. Lt.	1		1
8	Total Commissioned	14	15	29
9	WO		1	1

10	M/Sgt.	2		2
11	Sgt. 1st Cl	3		3
12	Sgt.	4		4
13	Cpl.	5		5
14	Pfc.	13		13
15	Pvt.			
16	Rct.			
17	Total Enlisted	27		27
18	Aggregate	41	16	57

By Order of the Governor:

                              JOHN H. MANNING
OFFICIAL: *Major General*
THOMAS B. LONGEST   *The Adjutant General*
Military Operations Officer
Adjutant General's Department

STATE OF NORTH CAROLINA
ADJUTANT GENERAL'S DEPARTMENT
RALEIGH

GENERAL ORDERS
No.   35   9 November 1951

AMENDMENT TO GENERAL ORDERS—So much of Par. 4, General Orders No. 32, this Department, dtd. 1 November 1951, as pertains to inactivation of Air Section, State Hq & Hq Detachment, NC NG as reads, "is inactivated this date," is amended to read "is inactivated effective 31 October 1951."

By Order of the Governor:

                              JOHN H. MANNING
OFFICIAL: *Major General*
THOMAS B. LONGEST   *The Adjutant General*
Military Operations Officer
The Adjutant General's Department

STATE OF NORTH CAROLINA
ADJUTANT GENERAL'S DEPARTMENT
RALEIGH

GENERAL ORDERS   26 November 1951
No.   36

SECTION I
REVOCATION OF GENERAL ORDERS

General Orders No. 34, this Department, dated 7 November 1951, pertaining to reorganization of Headquarters and Headquarters Detachment, North Carolina National Guard, effective 1 November 1951, is REVOKED.

SECTION II
REORGANIZATION OF STATE HQ AND HQ DETCH NCNG

PAC Ltr, NGB, NG-AROTO 325.4—N. C. (29 Oct 51), Subject: Table of Organization, State Headquarters and Headquarters Detachment, dated 15 November 1951, the State Headquarters and Headquarters Detachment, North Carolina National Guard, is reorganized in accordance with the following Table of Organization, effective 19 November 1951:

Line	Grade	National Guard	Augmentation For Selective Service	Total
1	Maj. Gen.			
2	Brig. Gen.	1		1
3	Colonel	2	2	4
4	Lt. Colonel	5	4	9
5	Major	2	7	9
6	Captain	3	2	5
7	1st. Lt.	1		1
8	Total Commissioned	14	15	29
9	WO		1	1
10	M/Sgt.	2		2
11	Sgt. 1st Cl	3		3
12	Sgt.	4		4
13	Cpl.	5		5
14	Pfc.	13		13
15	Pvt.			
16	Rct.			
17	Total Enlisted	27		27
18	Aggregate	41	16	57

By Order of the Governor:

OFFICIAL:
THOMAS B. LONGEST
Military Operations Officer
Adjutant General's Department

JOHN H. MANNING
Major General
The Adjutant General

STATE OF NORTH CAROLINA
ADJUTANT GENERAL'S DEPARTMENT
RALEIGH

GENERAL ORDERS   6 December 1951
No.   37

1. Pursuant to authority, The Chief, National Guard Bureau, on NGB Form 5, authority to organize National Guard units, Commanding Officer of the following unit, North Carolina National Guard, will proceed with enlistment of men for their respective commands, effective 19 November 1951.

REPORT OF THE ADJUTANT GENERAL

UNIT DESIGNATION	STATION	APPLICABLE T/O&E	REQUIRED FOR FEDERAL RECOGNITION		
			Off	WO	EM
121st Antiaircraft Artillery Operations Detachment.	Charlotte. N. C.	44-7 15 Oct. 48 W/Cl, 2 & 3 RT 44-7-22, 1 Jun. 49	2		15

2. WD NGB Form 21 is prescribed for use in enlistment of men. The original and two carbon copies will be prepared. No Oath of Enlistment will be dated prior to the effective date. Care will be exercised in the preparation of enlistment records; all questions carefully answered; proper and full information given, and all copies will be legible.

3. It is required to have a physical examination of each enlisted man, report of which will be prepared on NGB Form 21, in triplicate, (Reverse side of Enlistment Record). Physical examination may be made by medical officers of the Regular Army, National Guard officers, Reserve Corps, the Navy, U. S. Public Health Service, or by civilian physicians. Should none other than a civilian physician be available to make the physical examination, it is required that the name or names of a reputable physician of the community be submitted promptly to The State Adjutant General, who will report the name to the National Guard Bureau that he may be furnished a copy of the regulations prescribing the physical requirements for enlistment. The examining physician will be advised that Questions 56, Chest X-Ray and 57, Serology, are not required to be completed except in a case in which the condition of the man would deem to warrant the answer to such questions. It is not deemed necessary to await receipt of the regulations mentioned to begin the physical examination of men.

4. Before the enlistment of any man, the Recruiting Officer will carefully read NGR 25, dated 9 January 1947, and changes thereto. A number of local physicians within the State have offered to make the physical examination of enlisted men at a cost not to exceed $2.00 per man, and due to the availability of funds in the State budget, it is desired, if practicable, not to exceed this amount.

By Order of the Governor:

OFFICIAL:
THOMAS B. LONGEST
Military Operations Officer
Adjutant General's Department

JOHN H. MANNING
Major General
The Adjutant General

REPORT OF THE ADJUTANT GENERAL

STATE OF NORTH CAROLINA
ADJUTANT GENERAL'S DEPARTMENT
RALEIGH

GENERAL ORDERS   10 December 1951
No.   38

SECTION I
REVOCATION OF GENERAL ORDERS

General Orders No. 33, this Department, dated 5 November 1951, pertaining to the Field Training time for elements of Hq Hq Btry, IV Corps Arty, NCNG, for Summer Field Training 1951, is REVOKED.

SECTION II
AMENDMENT TO GENERAL ORDERS

PAC Amendment No. 2 to TA No. 31-B, NGB, dated 30 October 1951, so much of G. O. No. 22, this Department, dated 26 July 1951, as authorizes 16 days Field Training time for elements of Hq Hq Btry, IV Corps Arty, NCNG, is AMENDED to authorize 18 days for one (1) officer traveling by Government motor from home station, Midway Park, North Carolina, to Fort McClellan, Alabama. VOTAG, NC, 16 August 1951, for Lt Col KERMIT L. GUTHRIE, O-346619, Hq Hq Btry, IV Corps Arty, NCNG, to proceed from Midway Park, North Carolina to Fort McClellan, Alabama on 17 August 1951 and return to home station on 3 September 1951 as a member of the Advance and Rear Detachment for his unit is confirmed and made of record.

By Order of the Governor:

OFFICIAL:
THOMAS B. LONGEST
Military Operations Officer
Adjutant General's Department

JOHN H. MANNING
Major General
The Adjutant General

STATE OF NORTH CAROLINA
ADJUTANT GENERAL'S DEPARTMENT
RALEIGH

GENERAL ORDERS   13 December 1951
No.   39

SECTION I
AMENDMENT OF GENERAL ORDERS

So much of General Orders No. 37, this Department, dated 6 December 1951, pertaining to the organization of the 121st Antiaircraft Artillery Operations Detachment, NC. NG., as reads: "2 Officers and 15 EM required for Federal Recognition," is AMENDED, to read: "2 Officers and 7 EM required for Federal Recognition."

By Order of the Governor:

OFFICIAL:
THOMAS B. LONGEST
Military Operations Officer
Adjutant General's Department

JOHN H. MANNING
Major General
The Adjutant General

REPORT OF THE ADJUTANT GENERAL

GENERAL ORDERS
No. 40

31 December 1951

SECTION I
ORGANIZATION OF 8156TH AIR BASE SQUADRON, NCANG

1. Pursuant to the authority contained in letter NG AFOTP, National Guard Bureau, 16 November 1951, Subject: "Authorization for Air Base Squadron, North Carolina Air National Guard," the following unit is organized effective 1 January 1952.

Unit	*Location*
8156th Air Base Squadron North Carolina Air National Guard (T/D ANG 1-102 dated 1 November 1951)	Morris Field Charlotte, N. C.

2. Requirement for Federal recognition inspection is waived.

3. Concurrent with this organization, temporary additional military spaces authorized Headquarters, North Carolina Air National Guard as Air Base Flight B is withdrawn. Personnel and equipment now assigned to Air Base Flight B will be transferred to 8156th Air Base Squadron, effective 1 January 1952.

By Order of the Governor:

OFFICIAL:
THOMAS B. LONGEST
Military Operations Officer
Adjutant General's Department

JOHN H. MANNING
Major General
The Adjutant General

1952 GENERAL ORDERS

STATE OF NORTH CAROLINA
ADJUTANT GENERAL'S DEPARTMENT
RALEIGH

GENERAL ORDERS 16 January 1952
No. 1

Amendment of General Orders

So much of Paragraph 1, Section I, General Orders No. 40, this Department, 31 December 1951, pertaining to organization of 8156th Air Base Squadron, NCANG, as reads, "T/D ANG 1-10*2* dated 1 November 1951," is AMENDED to read, "T/D ANG 1-10*1* dated 1 November 1951."

By Order of the Governor:

JOHN H. MANNING
Major General
OFFICIAL
THOMAS B. LONGEST
Military Operations Officer
Adjutant General's Department
The Adjutant General

STATE OF NORTH CAROLINA
ADJUTANT GENERAL'S DEPARTMENT
RALEIGH

GENERAL ORDERS 25 January 1952
Number 2

Attachment of Unit

The 121st AAA Operations Detachment, NCNG, Charlotte, North Carolina, is attached to IV Corps Artillery, NCNG, Charlotte, North Carolina, effective 25 January 1952.

By Order of the Governor:

JOHN H. MANNING
Major General
OFFICIAL
THOMAS B. LONGEST
Military Operations Officer
Adjutant General's Department
The Adjutant General

STATE OF NORTH CAROLINA
ADJUTANT GENERAL'S DEPARTMENT
RALEIGH

GENERAL ORDERS 12 February 1952
No. 3

1. Pursuant to Sec. 93, National Defense Act, as amended and the provisions of Sec. II, National Guard Regulations 48, 4 October 1946, Annual Armory Inspections of the following North Carolina National Guard units will be conducted by officers of the Regular Army detailed by the Commanding General of the Third Army at the places and on the dates indicated:

Report of The Adjutant General

Unit	Location	Date	Inspector
Hq. & Hq. Co., 3d Bn., 119th Inf.	Clinton	10 Mar. 52	Lt. Col. R. E. McMurray
Hq. & Hq. Co., 2d Bn., 119th Inf.	Wilson	11 Mar. 52	Lt. Col. R. E. McMurray
Co. M, 119th Inf.	Warsaw	12 Mar. 52	Lt. Col. R. E. McMurray
Hq. & Hq. Btry., 196th FA Gp.	Kinston	20 Mar. 52	Lt. Col. R. E. McMurray

2. Armory Inspections will be made in two (2) parts: An administrative inspection of armory facilities, property, official records, and general administration. The organization commander, first sergeant, caretaker, supply sergeant and administrative assistant will be present at the armory at the time designated for the administrative inspection. There will also be an inspection of the state of training of all personnel of the organization and the adequacy of equipment. The time devoted to the training inspection should not exceed the time required in a normal armory drill period. The hours of these two parts of the inspection will be set by arrangement between the unit commander and the inspecting officer.

3. All property, arms, clothing and equipment will be thoroughly cleaned and put in good condition. Property in supply rooms and individual lockers will be neatly and carefully arranged, in order that the inspecting officer may check their condition without a loss of time.

4. Attendance at inspection is compulsory. A report of all absentees from inspection by reason of unavoidable causes, such as sickness, etc., will be rendered to the inspection officer. Absentee without leave of absence will be dealt with in accordance with the law.

5. The inspection will be formal. The unit commanders will review carefully Sec. II, NGR-48; SR 20-10-8, 21 July 1949, as amended, and present the unit for inspection according to the directives contained therein.

6. The expense enjoined is necessary in the military service.

By Order of the Governor:

OFFICIAL
THOMAS B. LONGEST
Military Operations Officer
Adjutant General's Department

JOHN H. MANNING
Major General
The Adjutant General

STATE OF NORTH CAROLINA
ADJUTANT GENERAL'S DEPARTMENT
RALEIGH

GENERAL ORDERS
No. 4

6 March 1952

1. Pursuant to Sec. 93, National Defense Act, as amended, and the provisions of Sec. II, National Guard Regulations 48, 4 October 1946, Annual Armory Inspections of the following North Carolina National Guard units will be conducted by officers of the Regular Army detailed by the Commanding General of the Third Army at the places and on the dates indicated:

Unit	Location	Date
Co. L, 119th Inf.	Goldsboro	31 Mar. 52
Co. G, 119th Inf.	Rocky Mount	1 Apr. 52
Med. Co., 119th Inf.	Wilson	2 Apr. 52

2. Armory Inspections will be made in two (2) parts: An administrative inspection of armory facilities, property, official records, and general administration. The organization commander, first sergeant, caretaker, supply sergeant and administrative assistant will be present at the armory at the time designated for the administrative inspection. There will also be an inspection of the state of training of all personnel of the organization and the adequacy of equipment. The time devoted to the training inspection should not exceed the time required in a normal armory drill period. The hours of these two parts of the inspection will be set by arrangement between the unit commander and the inspecting officer.

3. All property, arms, clothing and equipment will be thoroughly cleaned and put in good condition. Property in supply rooms and individual lockers will be neatly and carefully arranged, in order that the inspecting officer may check their condition without a loss of time.

4. Attendance at inspection is compulsory. A report of all absentees from inspection by reason of unavoidable causes, such as sickness, etc., will be rendered to the inspection officer. Absentee without leave of absence will be dealt with in accordance with the law.

5. The inspection will be formal. The unit commanders will review carefully Sec. II, NGR-48; SR 20-10-8, 21 July 1949, as amended, and present the unit for inspection according to the directives contained therein.

6. The expense enjoined is necessary in the military service.

By Order of the Governor:

OFFICIAL
THOMAS B. LONGEST
Military Operations Officer
Adjutant General's Department

JOHN H. MANNING
Major General
The Adjutant General

STATE OF NORTH CAROLINA
ADJUTANT GENERAL'S DEPARTMENT
RALEIGH

GENERAL ORDERS 19 March 1952
No. 5

1. Purusant to authority, Chief, National Guard Bureau, on NGB Form 5, Authority to Organize National Guard Units, Commanding Officer of the following unit, North Carolina National Guard, will proceed with enlistment of men for his respective command, effective 1 March 1952:

UNIT DESIGNATION	STATION	APPLICABLE T/O&E	REQUIRED FOR FEDERAL RECOGNITION		
			Off	WO	EM
Co. B, 167th MP Bn.............	Lasker, N. C........	19-37 15 Oct. 48 w/Cl & 2 RT 19-37-22 1 June 49.....	2	......	40

2. WD NGB Form 21 is prescribed for use in enlistment of men. The original and two carbon copies will be prepared. No Oath of Enlistment will be dated prior to the effective date. Care will be exercised in the preparation of enlistment records; all questions carefully answered, proper and full information given, and all copies will be legible.

3. It is required to have a physical examination of each enlisted man, report of which will be prepared on NGB Form 21, in triplicate, (Reverse side of Enlistment Record). Physical examination may be made by medical officers of the Regular Army, National Guard officers, Reserve Corps, the Navy, U. S. Public Health Service, or by civilian physicians. Should none other than a civilian physician be available to make the physical examination it is required that the name or names of a reputable physician of the community be submitted promptly to the Adjutant General, who will report the name to the National Guard Bureau that he may be furnished a copy of the regulations prescribing the physical requirements for enlistment. The examining physician will be advised that Questions 56, Chest X-Ray and 57, Serology, are not required to be completed except in a case in which the condition of the man would deem to warrant the answer to such questions. It is not deemed necessary to await receipt of the regulations mentioned to begin the physical examination of men.

4. Before the enlistment of any man, the Recruiting Officer will carefully read NGR 25, dated 9 January 1947, and changes thereto. A number of local physicians within the State have offered to make the physical examination of enlisted men at a cost not to exceed $2.00 per man, and due to the availability of funds in the State Budget, it is desired, if practicable, not to exceed this amount.

By Order of the Governor:

JOHN H. MANNING
Major General
The Adjutant General

OFFICIAL

THOMAS B. LONGEST
Military Operations Officer
Adjutant General's Department

REPORT OF THE ADJUTANT GENERAL

STATE OF NORTH CAROLINA
ADJUTANT GENERAL'S DEPARTMENT
RALEIGH

GENERAL ORDERS   28 March 1952
No.   6

1. Pursuant to authority, The Chief, National Guard Bureau, on NGB Form 5, Authority to Organize National Guard Units. Commanding Officer of the following unit, North Carolina National Guard, will proceed with enlistment of men for his respective command, effective 15 March 1952.

Unit Designation	Applicable T/O&E		Required for Federal Recognition			
			Off	Off & Wo	Wo	EM
Btry. D, 725th AAA AW Bn. (Mobile) Benson, North Carolina	44-27 w/Cl & 2 44-27-22	4 Oct. 48 1 June 49	------	2	------	30

2. WD NGB Form 21 is prescribed for use in enlistment of men. The original and two carbon copies will be prepared. No Oath of Enlistment will be dated prior to the effective date. Care will be exercised in the preparation of enlistment records; all questions carefully answered, proper and full information given, and all copies will be legible.

3. It is required to have a physical examination of each enlisted man, report of which will be prepared on NGB Form 21, in triplicate, (Reverse side of Enlistment Record). Physical examination may be made by medical officers of the Regular Army, National Guard officers, Reserve Corps, the Navy, U. S. Public Health Service, or by civilian physicians. Should none other than a civilian physician be available to make the physical examination it is required that the name or names of a reputable physician of the community be submitted promptly to the Adjutant General, who will report the name to the National Guard Bureau that he may be furnished a copy of the regulations prescribing the physical requirements for enlistment. The examining physician will be advised that Questions 56, Chest X-Ray, and 57, Serology, are not required to be completed except in a case in which the condition of the man would deem to warrant the answer to such questions. It is not deemed necessary to await receipt of the regulations mentioned to begin the physical examination of men.

4. Before the enlistment of any man, the Recruiting Officer will carefully read NGR 25, dated 9 January 1947, and changes thereto. A number of local physicians within the State have offered to make the physical examination of enlisted men at a cost not to exceed $2.00 per man, and due to the avail-

ability of funds in the State Budget, it is desired, if practicable, not to exceed this amount.

By Order of the Governor:

OFFICIAL
THOMAS B. LONGEST
Military Operations Officer
Adjutant General's Department

JOHN H. MANNING
Major General
The Adjutant General

STATE OF NORTH CAROLINA
ADJUTANT GENERAL'S DEPARTMENT
RALEIGH

GENERAL ORDERS   16 April 1952
No.   7

1. Pursuant to Sec. 93, National Defense Act, as amended, and the provisions of Sec. II, National Guard Regulations 48, 4 October 1946, Annual Armory Inspections of the following North Carolina National Guard units will be conducted by officers of the Regular Army detailed by the Commanding General of the Third Army at the places and on the dates indicated:

Unit	Location	Date	Inspector
Svc. Co., 120th Inf.	Asheville, N. C.	20 May 1952	Lt. Col. R. E. McMurray
30th Signal Company	Canton, N. C.	21 May 1951	Lt. Col. R. E. McMurray
Mdm. Tk. Co., 120th Inf.	Waynesville, N. C.	22 May 1952	Lt. Col. R. E. McMurray

2. Armory Inspections will be made in two (2) parts: an administrative inspection of armory facilities, property, official records, and general administration. The organization commander, first sergeant, caretaker, supply sergeant and administrative assistant will be present at the armory at the time designated for the administrative inspection. There will also be an inspection of the state of training of all personnel of the organization and the adequacy of equipment. The time devoted to the training inspection should not exceed the time required in a normal armory drill period. The hours of these two parts of the inspection will be set by arrangement between the unit commander and the inspecting officer.

3. All property, arms, clothing and equipment will be thoroughly cleaned and put in good condition. Property in supply rooms and individual lockers will be neatly and carefully arranged, in order that the inspecting officer may check their condition without loss of time.

4. Attendance at inspection is compulsory. A report of all absentees from inspection by reason of unavoidable causes, such as sickness, etc., will be rendered to the inspecting officer. Absentees without leave of absence will be dealt with in accordance with the law.

5. The inspection will be formal. The unit commanders will review care-

fully Sec. II, NGR-48; SR 20-10-8, 21 July 1949, as amended, and present the unit for inspection according to the directives contained therein.

6. The expense enjoined is necessary in the military service.

By Order of the Governor:

OFFICIAL
THOMAS B. LONGEST
Military Operations Officer
Adjutant General's Department

JOHN H. MANNING
Major General
The Adjutant General

STATE OF NORTH CAROLINA
ADJUTANT GENERAL'S DEPARTMENT
RALEIGH

GENERAL ORDERS
No. 8

23 May 1952

1. PAC Letter, NGB, NG-AROTO 325.4 General, Subject: "Redesignation and Reorganization of National Guard Nondivisional Antiaircraft Artillery Units," dated 7 May 1952, the 217th Radio Controlled Airplane Target Detachment, North Carolina National Guard, is hereby redesignated and reorganized in accordance with T/O&E indicated below, effective 1 June 1952. Maximum authorized strength for officers and enlisted men is listed in Column 7 of appropriate T/O&E:

New Designation	*Old Designation*	*T/O&E & Date*
217th Antiaircraft Artillery Detachment (Radio Controlled Airplane Target)	217th Radio Controlled Airplane Target Detachment	44-8A 15 Mar 52

2. The provisions of NGB Circular No. 22, dated 24 September 1948, apply to this reorganization.

By Order of the Governor:

OFFICIAL
THOMAS B. LONGEST
Military Operations Officer
Adjutant General's Department

JOHN H. MANNING
Major General
The Adjutant General

STATE OF NORTH CAROLINA
ADJUTANT GENERAL'S DEPARTMENT
RALEIGH

GENERAL ORDERS
No. 9

2 June 1952

1. PAC Section 94 NDA and TA No. 31, with amendments 1 & 2, NGB, dated 21 April, 15 May and 21 May 1952, respectively, NCNG organizations listed herein will mobilize at home stations and w/p to Camp Stewart, Georgia for

Report of The Adjutant General

Field Training during the period 15 June 1952 to 29 June 1952, inclusive. Upon completion of Field Training, unless sooner relieved by proper authority, return to home stations:

    Hq Hq Btry 252nd AAA Gp
    725th AAA AW Bn Mbl
    130th AAA AW Bn (SP)
    94th Army Band
    123rd Signal Radar Maint Unit, Type C
    217th AAA Detachment (RCAT)
    3624th Ord Med Maint Co, 1 officer
    1st Lt James M. Fletcher, 0-2042881
    121st AAA Opn Detachment
    Hq 30th Inf Div (In Part) 1 officer
    1st Lt Luther W. Clark, 0-961855

All troops listed above not assigned to the 252nd AAA Group are attached to the 252nd AAA Group for Administration, Supply and Training for the Field Training period. Detachments authorized are as follows:

        Advance Detachment   13-14 June 1952
            9 Officers—56 Enlisted Men

        Rear Detachment 30 June 1952
            9 Officers—56 Enlisted Men

    Pre-Camp Mess School Detachment   11-14 June 1952
            2 Officers—23 Enlisted Men
(Personnel to be listed by name in separate order this Department)

        Camp Supply Detachment   12-30 June 1952
            1 Officer—2 Enlisted Men
Major John E. Farmer, 0-1040708, 252nd AAA Gp, Wilmington, N. C.
SFC John W. Willetts, 25011241, 252nd AAA Gp, Wilmington, N. C.
Sgt Edwin L. West, 25011231, 252nd AAA Gp, Wilmington, N. C.

Motor Convoy Detachment—3 days—(2 days advance and 1 day rear)
            1 Officer—44 Enlisted Men

The Commanding Officer, 252nd AAA Group, after consultation with those concerned, will designate personnel for the advance, rear and motor convoy detachments. In compliance with Par. 36, NGR-45, units will take to Camp at least 50% of officers and 60% of enlisted strength.

2. *Transportation:* a. Travel to and from Camp will be conducted as a troop movement. The maximum use will be made of all Government owned motor vehicles to transport both personnel and organizational equipment. Motor convoys will proceed under the direction and command of the Senior Officer or an officer designated by him as convoy commander. All Federal regulations and state and local laws will be complied with. March orders covering motor convoys will be issued by organizations concerned. Copies of these orders will be furnished this Department and Headquarters, 252nd AAA Group. For rail and/or bus movements see Field Training Circular No. 7, Office of Acting USP & DO for North Carolina, dated 26 May 1952. Lt

Col William Lamont, Jr., 0-385712, Arty, and Major Joseph E. Boylan, Jr., 0-422001, Arty, are designated Train Commanders and will assume command and responsibility for train and troops thereon. Provisions of TM 55-590, March 1947, will be complied with. Train Commanders will furnish such reports as the USP & DO for North Carolina and the Transportation Officer, Camp Stewart, Georgia may require. The following officers are designated as Transportation Officers, in addition to their other duties, for the entraining points listed:

   Capt Walter R. Bullock, 0-1040503 Fayetteville, N. C.
   Hq Hq Btry 130th AAA AW Bn, NCNG

   Capt Simeon T. Enzor, 0-814671   Fair Bluff, N. C.
   Btry B, 725th AAA AW Bn, NCNG

   Capt Harold A. Waldron, 0-1048230 Whiteville, N. C.
   Hq Hq Btry 725th AAA AW Bn, NCNG

   Capt Osborne K. Walls, 0-1047832 Wilmington, N. C.
   Hq Hq Btry 252nd AAA Gp, NCNG

Regardless of means employed, the amount of equipment and impedimenta transported to and from field training camp will be strictly limited to training essentials to include athletic equipment but not day room furniture and equipment. TR to be issued by Acting USP & DO, North Carolina for all rail and bus movements. Travel of dependents not authorized.

 b. Personnel authorized to travel by privately owned vehicle will be covered in separate order.

 3. *Pay*: a. Regular payrolls will be submitted to the USP & DO for North Carolina, who will accomplish the certificate on the payrolls as to the availability of funds. The rolls will be paid by the designated Finance Officer, Camp Stewart, Georgia, and payment will be made in cash. The Acting USP & DO, North Carolina, will settle all accounts incident to the Camp payable from Federal funds.

 b. Detachment payrolls will be prepared covering the periods authorized for the advance and motor convoy detachments by organizations listed in Par. 1 above. Similar rolls will be prepared for the rear detachments. These rolls will be briefed to show whether the detachment is advance, rear or motor convoy and the organization to which it pertains. The unit to which each individual belongs will be clearly shown in the body of the roll. Personnel of these detachments will be paid for the period of the encampment proper on the regular payroll of their unit. The detachment payrolls cover only the period of additional duty as members of the advance, rear or motor convoy detachments. Two payrolls will be prepared for motor convoy detachment, one for the advance element and one for the rear element.

 c. The Pre-Camp Mess School Detachment—Mess personnel payroll will be prepared by Hq, 252nd AAA Group for all personnel attending.

 d. Camp Supply Detachment—Personnel on this Detachment will be paid on one roll, prepared by Hq, 252nd AAA Group, for the entire period authorized the Detachment.

4. *Subsistence*: The provisions of Par. 15, NGB Ltr, NG-ARL 354.1 Gen, Subject: "Administrative Instructions for Field Training of the National Guard (Army units) Calendar Year 1952," dated 1 January 1952, will apply. The travel rations at a total value of $2.50 per day, not to exceed $1.00 per meal, is authorized for the period of travel only. The number of meals entitled to while traveling, and their purchase, will be as prescribed in Field Training Circular No. 5, Acting USP & DO, N. C., dated 8 May 1952. Messes while in Camp will be established as directed by Commanding Officers, 252nd AAA Group. An officer messing at enlisted men's mess at Camp, or with enlisted men during the period of travel to and from Camp, will be charged per day as follows regardless of the type of rations furnished:

One Meal	Two Meals	Three Meals
45¢	$1.35	$1.35

5. At termination of Camp, the Commanding Officer, 252nd AAA Group, will submit to TAG, NC a report on the Camp with such recommendations and comments as he may deem advisable.

6. Orders and regulations in force at Camp will be complied with by all concerned.

7. No debts or obligations against the State of North Carolina or the Federal Government will be incurred by any officer, enlisted man, or organization of the North Carolina National Guard except as authorized by this Department.

8. TDN: TBGAA 212/32060 18-1131 P1110-01 S31-079
              212/32060 18-1431 P1140-08 S31-079
              212/32060 18-1631 P1160-02 S31-079
              212/32060 18-2131 P1212-08 S31-079
              212/32060 18-2331 P1221-99 S31-079
              2122020   18-6731 P1670-07 S31-079

By Order of the Governor:

OFFICIAL
THOMAS B. LONGEST
Military Operations Officer
Adjutant General's Department

JOHN H. MANNING
Major General
The Adjutant General

STATE OF NORTH CAROLINA
ADJUTANT GENERAL'S DEPARTMENT
RALEIGH

GENERAL ORDERS　　　　　　　　　　　　　　　　　　　　　　　　　　　　4 June 1952
No.　　10

1. PAC Letter, NGB, NG-AROTO 325.4 General, Subject: "Reorganization of National Guard Antiaircraft Artillery Units (Nondivisional)," dated 28 May 1952, the Hq & Hq Btry, 252nd Antiaircraft Artillery Group, North Carolina National Guard, is hereby reorganized in accordance with T/O&E indicated below, *effective 1 July 1952*. Maximum authorized strength for officers

and warrant officers is listed in Column 7 and enlisted strength in Column 8 of appropriate T/O&E:

Unit & Designation	T/O&E & Date		Unit Structure	
	No.	Date	Orgn	Equip
Hq. &Hq. Btry, 252nd AAA Group......	44–12A	10 Apr. 52	Column 7 Sec. II	Column 5 Sec. III

2. The provisions of NGB Circular No. 22, dated 24 September 1948, apply to this reorganization.

3. The number of grades for each MOS, as shown in column 16 through 21 inclusive (Section II (Organization)) of all tables are authorized provided the total enlisted strength does not exceed the total shown in column 8. Personnel rendered surplus by this reorganization will be governed by the provisions of paragraph 6, NGR 15 and paragraph 20, NGR 130.

4. Since the T/O&E referred to above includes a Section III (Equipment) and such Section contains a full strength allowance column (column 4) and a reduced strength allowance column (column 5), National Guard Reduction Tables now being followed (for equipment only) will no longer be required nor be in effect on and after the date of reorganization.

By Order of the Governor:

OFFICIAL
THOMAS B. LONGEST
Military Operations Officer
Adjutant General's Department

JOHN H. MANNING
Major General
The Adjutant General

STATE OF NORTH CAROLINA
ADJUTANT GENERAL'S DEPARTMENT
RALEIGH

GENERAL ORDERS
No.   11

10 June 1952

1. PAC Section 94 NDA and TA No. 31-B, dated 7 May 1952, as amended by Amendment No. 1, dated 3 June 1952, DA & AF, NGB, NCNG organizations listed herein will mobilize at home stations and w/p to Fort McClellan, Alabama for Field Training during the period 6 July 1952 to 20 July 1952, inclusive. Upon completion of Field Training, unless sooner relieved by proper authority, return to home stations:

Unit

Hq Hq Detch, NCNG (Army Sec-Plus 1 W. O. from Selective Service Section)
Hq 30th Inf Div (In Part)
Hq Co 30th Inf Div
Med Detch 30th Inf Div
30th Signal Co
119th Inf

REPORT OF THE ADJUTANT GENERAL 59

120th Inf
112th FA Bn
113th FA Bn
Hq Hq Btry 30th Div Arty (In Part)
167th MP Bn

All non-divisional troops listed above are attached to the 30th Infantry Division for administration, supply and training during the Field Training period. Detachments authorized are as follows:

Advance and Rear Detachments are authorized not to exceed a maximum total of 855 man days; 10% of total man days authorized may be officer personnel. (No. personnel authorized each unit as listed in Summer Camp Memorandum No. 1-52, Hq, 30th Inf Div, dtd 28 April 1952)

Pre-Camp Mess School Detachment—2-5 July 1952

3 officers—111 enlisted men

(Personnel listed by name in Par. 1, SO No. 169, AGD, NC, dated 12 June 1952)

Camp Supply Detachment—1-28 July 1952

Name and Rank	SN	Unit
Capt. Richard G. York	0-1951365	Hq. & Hq. Detch, NCNG
Sgt. James P. Roberts	34313531	Hq. & Hq. Detch, NCNG
Cpl. George W. Harrison	24960037	Hq. & Hq. Detch, NCNG

One (1) Motor Convoy Detachment—5 days (3 days advance and 2 days rear)
7 officers—241 enlisted men

One (1) Motor Convoy Detachment—3 days (2 days advance and 1 day rear)
5 officers—153 enlisted men

In compliance with Par. 36, NGR 45, units will take to Camp at least 50% of officers and 60% of enlisted strength.

2. *Transportation*: a. Travel to and from Camp will be conducted as a troop movement. The maximum use will be made of all Government-owned motor vehicles and Army aircraft to transport both personnel and organizational equipment. Motor convoys will proceed under the direction and command of the Senior Officer or an officer designated by him as convoy commander. All Federal regulations and state and local laws will be complied with. March orders covering motor convoys will be issued by organizations concerned. Copies of these orders will be furnished this Department and Headquarters, 30th Infantry Division. For rail and/or bus movements, including shuttle movements, see Field Training Circular No. 9, Acting USP & DO for North Carolina, dated 9 June 1952. The following officers are designated Train Commanders and will assume command and responsibility for their trains and troops thereon:

Train No.	Rank, Name & SN	Station
Advance Detachment	Major William E. Ingram, O-532080	Elizabeth City, N. C.
1	Major John E. Floyd, O-401430	Warrenton, N. C.
2	Lt. Col. Edward F. Yarborough, O-1171421	Louisburg, N. C.
3	Lt. Col. Bernice A. Peterson, O-304079	Ahoskie, N. C.
4	Capt. Roswell K. Porter, O-1580178	Asheville, N. C.
5	Capt. Eugene A. Robbins, Jr., O-753305	Concord, N. C.
6	Capt. Conrad M. Blalock, O-809511	Winston-Salem, N. C.
7	Major Edward J. Winstead, O-1287109	Wilson, N. C.
8	Major Harper K. Sanders, Jr., O-415469	Durham, N. C.
9	Lt. Col. Tom Presnell, O-345783	Asheboro, N. C.
10	Major William M. Buck, O-1310353	Warsaw, N. C.

Provisions of TM 55-590, March 1947, will be complied with. Train Commanders will furnish such reports as the Transportation Officer, Fort McClellan, Alabama, or the USP & DO for North Carolina, may require. Regardless of means employed, the amount of equipment and impedimenta transported to and from Field Training camps will be strictly limited to training essentials to include athletic equipment but not day room furniture and equipment. TR to be issued by Acting USP & DO, North Carolina, for all rail and bus movements. Travel of dependents not authorized.

b. Personnel authorized travel by privately-owned vehicle will be covered in separate order.

c. The following officers are designated as Transportation Officers, in addition to their other duties, for the detachments or entraining points listed:

Capt Hubert E. Pennington, O-1996353
(Adv Detch only)
Raleigh, N. C.

Major William E. Ingram, O-532080
(Adv Detch only)
Elizabeth City, N. C.

1st Lt John P. Daughtry, O-1999152
(Adv Detch only)
Apex, N. C.

Capt Albert G. Taylor, O-985008
(Adv Detch only)
Charlotte, N. C.

CWO Woodrow B. Martin, W-2119660
(Adv Detch only)
Asheville, N. C.

1st Lt Admiral D. Waters, Jr., O-969986
Co B 167th MP Bn
Co E 119th Inf
Roanoke Rapids, N. C.

Capt Samuel T. Arrington, O-2037114
Co B 119th Inf
Warrenton, N. C.

Capt Scott P. Cooper, O-415169
Co C 119th Inf
Co A 119th Inf
Henderson, N. C.

Capt Melvin C. Holmes, O-1822276
Hq Hq Btry 113th FA Bn
Franklinton, N. C.

1st Lt Wiley Brown, 0-999659   Youngsville, N. C.
Svc Btry 113th FA Bn

Capt Robert E. H. Shelden, 0-1116002   Raleigh, N. C.
Hq 30th Inf Div (In Part)
Btry A 113th FA Bn

Capt Jay L. Ashley, 0-1578122   Apex, N. C.
Hq Co 30th Inf Div
Med Detch 30th Inf Div

1st Lt Columbus L. Bennett, 0-695295   Ahoskie, N. C.
Hq Hq Co 167th MP Bn
Co A 167th MP Bn
Hv Mortar Co 119th Inf

Capt Shelton G. Scott, 0-1583642   Fort McClellan, Ala.
Svc Co 119th Inf (Return to home station only)

Capt Oscar L. Smith, 0-1105831   Tarboro, N. C.
Co F 119th Inf

1st Lt Hiram J. Cuthrell, 0-967251   Rocky Mount, N. C.
Co G 119th Inf
Co H 119th Inf

Capt Roger F. Hall, 0-368924   Parkton, N. C.
Tank Co (Med) 119th Inf

Capt Charles R. Wanzer, 0-731240   Newton, N. C.
Co I 120th Inf

Capt William H. VanderLinden, Jr., 0-1286927   Hickory, N. C.
Co H 120th Inf

1st Lt John L. Wiltshire, 0-947672   Morganton, N. C.
Co L 120th Inf

Capt Roswell K. Porter, 0-1580178   Asheville, N. C.
Svc Co 120th Inf

Capt Samuel A. Carswell, 0-1292474   Waynesville, N. C.
Tank Co (Med) 120th Inf

2nd Lt Jack H. Russell, 0-997457   Canton, N. C.
Sig Co, 30th Inf Div

Capt William S. Murdoch, 0-1030237   Salisbury, N. C.
Co G 120th Inf
Co F 120th Inf

Capt Eugene A. Robbins, Jr., 0-753305   Concord, N. C.
Co E 120th Inf

Capt. William F. Harris, 0-1327144   Gastonia, N. C.
Co K 120th Inf

Capt Conrad M. Blalock, 0-809511   Winston-Salem, N. C.
Hq Hq Co 1st Bn 120th Inf
Co B 120th Inf
Co D 120th Inf

Capt Hugh A. Lagle, 0-843186   Mocksville, N. C.
Med Co 120th Inf

Capt Samuel H. Houston, 0-1290072   Kings Mountain, N. C.
Hq Hq Co 3rd Bn 120th Inf
Co M 120th Inf

1st Lt Richard A. Cook, 0-959109   Wilson, N. C.
Hq Hq Co 2nd Bn 119th Inf
Med Co 119th Inf

1st Lt Edward H. Wade, 0-988823   Dunn, N. C.
Btry B 113th FA Bn

Capt James T. Sanford, 0-1325525   Fayetteville, N. C.
Co K 119th Inf

Capt Stewart M. Pickett, 0-1290122   Durham, N. C.
Hq Hq Co 119th Inf
Hq Hq Co 1st Bn 119th Inf
Co D 119th Inf
Btry C 113th FA Bn

Capt David F. Davis, 0-1298644   Burlington, N. C.
Co A 120th Inf

Capt James R. Meador, 0-408505   Reidsville, N. C.
Hq Hq Co 120th Inf
Hv Mtr Co 120th Inf

Capt Beamer H. Barnes, 0-1043858   Lexington, N. C.
Co C 120th Inf
Hq Hq Co 2nd Bn 120th Inf

Capt James C. Kannan, Jr., 0-551075   Goldsboro, N. C.
Co L 119th Inf

1st Lt Henry C. Merritt, 0-947667   Warsaw, N. C.
Co M 119th Inf
Hq Hq Co 3rd Bn 119th Inf

1st Lt James H. Morse, 0-1303759   Wilmington, N. C.
Co I 119th Inf

3. *Pay*: a. Regular payrolls will be submitted to the USP & DO for North Carolina, who will accomplish the certificate on the payrolls as to the availability of funds. The rolls will be paid by the designated Finance Officer, Fort McClellan, Alabama, and payment will be made in cash. The Acting USP & DO, North Carolina, will settle all accounts incident to the Camp payable from Federal funds.

b. Detachment payrolls will be prepared covering the periods authorized for the advance and motor convoy detachments by organizations listed in Par. 1 above. Similar rolls will be prepared for the rear detachments. These rolls will be briefed to show whether the detachment is advance, rear or motor convoy and the organization to which it pertains. The unit to which each individual belongs will be clearly shown in the body of the roll. Personnel of these detachments will be paid for the period of the encampment proper on the regular payroll of their unit. The detachment payrolls cover only the period of additional duty as members of the advance, rear or motor convoy detachments. Two payrolls will be prepared for motor convoy detachment, one for the advance element and one for the rear element.

c. The Pre-Camp Mess School Detachment—Mess personnel payroll will be prepared by Hq, 30th Infantry Division for all personnel attending.

d. Camp Supply Detachment—Personnel on this Detachment will be paid on one roll, prepared by Hq & Hq Detch, for the entire period authorized the Detachment.

4. *Subsistence*: The provisions of Par. 15, NGB Ltr, NG-ARL 354.1 General, Subject: "Administrative Instructions for Field Training of the National Guard (Army Units) Calendar Year 1952," dated 1 January 1952, will apply. The travel rations at a total value of $2.50 per day; not to exceed $1.00 per meal, is authorized for the period of travel only. The number of meals entitled to while traveling, and their purchase, will be as prescribed in Field Training Circular No. 5, Acting USP & DO, N. C., dated 8 May 1952. Messes while in Camp will be established as directed by Commanding General, 30th Infantry Division. An officer messing at enlisted men's mess at Camp, or with enlisted men during the period of travel to and from Camp, will be charged per day as follows regardless of the type of rations furnished:

One Meal	Two Meals	Three Meals
45¢	$1.35	$1.35

5. At termination of Camp, the Commanding General, 30th Infantry Division (In Part), will submit to The Adjutant General, North Carolina, a report on the Camp with such recommendations and comments as he may deem advisable.

6. Orders and regulations in force at Camp will be complied with by all concerned.

7. No debts or obligations against the State of North Carolina or the Federal Government will be incurred by any officer, enlisted man, or organization of the North Carolina National Guard except as authorized by this Department.

8. TDN: TBGAA TBMAA 212/32060 18-1731 P1110-01 S31-079
                     212/32060 18-1831 P1140-08 S31-079
                     212/32060 18-1931 P1160-02 S31-079
                     212/32060 18-2431 P1212-08 S31-079
                     212/32060 18-2731 P1221-99 S31-079
                     2132020 18-6731 P1670-07 S31-079

By Order of the Governor:

OFFICIAL
WILLARD R. BLOXTON
Military Executive Officer
Adjutant General's Department

JOHN H. MANNING
Major General
The Adjutant General

STATE OF NORTH CAROLINA
ADJUTANT GENERAL'S DEPARTMENT
RALEIGH

GENERAL ORDERS   25 June 1952
No.   12

1. PAC Section 94 NDA and TA No. 31-C and 31-D, NGB, dated 7 May 1952, personnel of Selective Service Section, Hq & Hq Detachment, NCNG, will mobilize at home station and w/p to North Carolina Headquarters, Selective Service System, Raleigh North Carolina, for Field Training during the periods indicated below:

Rank and Name	SN	Station	Dates
Major Charles B. Ratchford	0-1281802	Raleigh, N. C.	6–20 July 1952
Capt. Thomas C. Brown	0-918758	Raleigh, N. C.	6–20 July 1952
Capt. Isaac T. Avery, Jr.	0-453401	Statesville, N. C.	6–20 July 1952
1st Lt. Grayson Hayes	0-981830	Raleigh, N. C.	6–20 July 1952
Col. Charles R. Jonas	0-224860	Lincolnton, N. C.	20 July-3 Aug. 1952
Major Lee Roy W. Armstrong	0-966576	Chapel Hill, N. C.	20 July-3 Aug. 1952
1st Lt. Stuart W. Sechriest	0-961813	Chapel Hill, N. C.	20 July-3 Aug. 1952

Upon completion of Field Training, unless sooner relieved by proper authority, will return to home stations.

2. *Pay:* Payroll will be submitted to the Acting USP & DO, North Carolina, and payment will be made by check by the Finance Officer, USA, Atlanta, Georgia.

3. At termination of Field Training, the Commanding Officer will submit a report to The Adjutant General, North Carolina, with such recommendations and comments as he may deem advisable.

4. TR to be issued by Acting USP & DO, North Carolina, where authorized.

5. No debts or obligations against the State of North Carolina or the Federal Government will be incurred except as authorized by this Department.

Report of The Adjutant General

6. TDN 212/32060 18-1731 P1110-01 S31-079
    212/32060 18-2731 P1221-99 S31-079

By Order of the Governor:

OFFICIAL
WILLARD R. BLOXTON
Military Executive Officer
Adjutant General's Department

JOHN H. MANNING
Major General
The Adjutant General

STATE OF NORTH CAROLINA
ADJUTANT GENERAL'S DEPARTMENT
RALEIGH

GENERAL ORDERS
No. 13

25 June 1952

1. PAC Section 94 NDA and TA No. 31-A, NGB, dated 21 April 1952, as amended, NCNG organizations listed herein will mobilize at home stations and w/p to Fort McClellan, Alabama for Field Training during the period 13 July 1952 to 27 July 1952, inclusive. Upon completion of Field Training, unless sooner relieved by proper authority, return to home stations:

Unit
Hq & Hq Btry, IV Corps Arty
Hq & Hq Btry, 252nd FA Gp
Hq & Hq Btry, 196th FA Gp
505th FA Bn
3624th Ord Med Maint Co

The 3624th Ord Med Maint Co is attached to Hq, IV Corps Artillery for administration, supply and training for the Field Training period. In compliance with Par. 36, NGR 45, units will take to Camp at least 50% of officers and 60% of enlisted strength.

2. *Detachments*: The Commanding General, IV Corps Artillery, will designate personnel for the authorized detachments listed below, except Pre-Camp Mess School Detachment. Personnel of this Detachment are listed in Par. 1, SO No. 177, AGD, NC, dated 23 June 1952.

Advance Detachment: Not to exceed a maximum total of 134 man days; 10% of total man days authorized may be officer personnel.

Motor Convoy Detachments:
One (1) Motor Convoy Detachment—3 days (2 days advance—1 officer 30 enlisted men; 1 day rear—1 officer 48 enlisted men)

One (1) Motor Convoy Detachment—5 days (3 days advance—2 officers 47 enlisted men; 2 days rear—2 officers 48 enlisted men)

Pre-Camp Mess School Detachment—9-12 July 1952
2 officers   19 enlisted men

Camp Supply Detachment—10-12 July 1952
1 officer   2 enlisted men

3. *Transportation*: a. Travel to and from Camp will be conducted as a troop movement. The maximum use will be made of all Government-owned motor vehicles and Army aircraft to transport both personnel and organizational equipment. Motor convoys will proceed under the direction and command of the Senior Officer or an officer designated by him as convoy commander. All Federal regulations and state and local laws will be complied with. March orders covering motor convoys will be issued by organizations concerned. Copies of these orders will be furnished this Department and Headquarters, IV Corps Artillery. For rail and/or bus movements, including shuttle movements, see Field Training Circular No. 9, Acting USP & DO for North Carolina, dated 9 June 1952. The following officers are designated Train Commanders and will assume command and responsibility for their trains and the troops thereon:

Main No.	Rank, Name & SN	Station
5067	Major Linley W. Gerringer, Jr., O-1168246	Greensboro, N. C.
5068	Major George H. Friddle, 0-577605	Charlotte, N. C.
5069	Lt. Col. Guy C. Langston, 0-417740	Kinston, N. C.

Provisions of TM 55-590, March 1947, will be complied with. Train Commanders will furnish such reports as the Transportation Officer, Fort McClellan, Alabama, or the USP & DO for North Carolina, may require. Regardless of means employed, the amount of equipment and impedimenta transported to and from Field Training camps will be strictly limited to training essentials to include athletic equipment but not day room furniture and equipment. TR to be issued by Acting USP & DO, North Carolina, for all rail and bus movements. Travel of dependents not authorized.

b. Personnel authorized travel by privately owned vehicle will be covered in separate order.

c. The following officers are designated as Transportation Officers, in addition to their other duties, for organizations or entraining points listed:

2nd Lt Kenneth E. Lewis, 0-998004   Greensboro, N. C.
Hq & Hq Btry 252nd FA Gp
505th FA Bn
3624th Ord Med Maint Co

2nd Lt Jimmie B. Huggins, 0-393917   Charlotte, N. C.
Hq & Hq Btry, IV Corps Arty

Capt Thomas W. Simmons, 0-961588   Kinston, N. C.
Hq & Hq Btry 196th FA Gp

4. *Pay*: a. Regular payrolls will be submitted to the USP & DO for North Carolina, who will accomplish the certificate on the payrolls as to the availability of funds. The rolls will be paid by the designated Finance Officer, Fort McClellan, Alabama, and payment will be made in cash. The Acting

USP & DO, North Carolina, will settle all accounts incident to the Camp payable from Federal funds.

b. Detachment payrolls will be prepared covering the periods authorized for the advance and motor convoy detachments by organizations listed in Par. 1 above. Similar rolls will be prepared for the rear detachments. These rolls will be briefed to show whether the detachment is advance, rear or motor convoy and the organization to which it pertains. The unit to which each individual belongs will be clearly shown in the body of the roll. Personnel of these detachments will be paid for the period of the encampment proper on the regular payroll of their unit. The detachment payrolls cover only the period of additional duty as members of the advance, rear or motor convoy detachments. Two payrolls will be prepared for motor convoy detachment, one for the advance element and one for the rear element.

c. The Pre-Camp Mess School Detachment—Mess personnel payroll will be prepared by Hq, IV Corps Artillery, for all personnel attending.

d. Camp Supply Detachment—Personnel on this Detachment will be paid on one roll, prepared by Hq, IV Corps Artillery, for the entire period authorized the Detachment.

5. *Subsistence*: The provisions of Par. 15, NGB Ltr, NG-ARL 354.1 General. Subject: "Administrative Instructions for Field Training of the National Guard (Army Units) Calendar Year 1952," dated 1 January 1952, will apply. The travel rations at a total value of $2.50 per day, not to exceed $1.00 per meal, is authorized for the period of travel only. The number of meals entitled to while traveling, and their purchase, will be as prescribed in Field Training Circular No. 5, Acting USP & DO, N. C., dated 8 May 1952. Messes while in Camp will be established as directed by Commanding General, IV Corps Artillery. An officer messing at enlisted men's mess at Camp, or with enlisted men during the period of travel to and from Camp, will be charged per day as follows regardless of type of rations furnished:

One Meal	Two Meals	Three Meals
45¢	$1.35	$1.35

6. At termination of Camp, the Commanding General, IV Corps Artillery, will submit to The Adjutant General, North Carolina, a report on the Camp with such recommendations and comments as he may deem advisable.

7. Orders and regulations in force at Camp will be complied with by all concerned.

8. No debts or obligations against the State of North Carolina or the Federal Government will be incurred by any officer, enlisted man or organization of the North Carolina National Guard except as authorized by this Department.

9. TDN: TBGAA TBMAA 212/32060 18-1731 P1110-01 S31-079
212/32060 18-1831 P1140-08 S31-079
212/32060 18-1931 P1160-02 S31-079
212/32060 18-2431 P1212-08 S31-079
212/32060 18-2731 P1221-99 S31-079
2132020 18-6731 P1670-07 S31-079

By Order of the Governor:

OFFICIAL
WILLARD R. BLOXTON
Military Executive Officer
Adjutant General's Department

JOHN H. MANNING
Major General
The Adjutant General

STATE OF NORTH CAROLINA
ADJUTANT GENERAL'S DEPARTMENT
RALEIGH

GENERAL ORDERS
No. 14

26 June 1952

SECTION I
Re-establishment of the 156th Fighter Interceptor Squadron, North Carolina Air National Guard

1. Pursuant to authority contained in Letter, National Guard Bureau, NG-AFOTP, Subject: "Re-establishment of the 156th Fighter-Interceptor Squadron, North Carolina Air National Guard," dated 4 June 1952, the re-establishment of the 156th Fighter-Interceptor Squadron, North Carolina Air National Guard, station Morris Field, Charlotte, North Carolina, is announced, effective 10 July 1952, under the following T/O's:

        T/O 1-1256P, 1 x Part II, 1 Dec 51
        T/O 1-7504P, 1 x Part IIB, 1 Dec 51
        T/O 1-7502P, 1 x Part IIB, 1 Dec 51
        T/O 1-8504P, 1 x Part IIA, 1 Dec 51
        T/O 1-8013P, 1 x Part IIA, 1 Dec 51
        T/O 1-8024P, 1 x Part IIA, 1 Jan 52
        T/O 1-8015, 1 x Part IIEA, 1 Jan 52
        T/O 1-8503P, 1 x Part IIA, 1 Dec 51
        T/O 1-9022, 1 x Part IIAD, 1 Jan 52

2. Concurrently with the re-establishment of the 156th Fighter-Interceptor Squadron, the 8156th Air Base Squadron will be discontinued and personnel and equipment transferred to the 156th Squadron. The 156th Fighter-Interceptor Squadron is authorized to recruit its full strengths authorized under the above T/O's.

By Order of the Governor:

OFFICIAL
WILLARD R. BLOXTON
Military Executive Officer
Adjutant General's Department

JOHN H. MANNING
Major General
The Adjutant General

REPORT OF THE ADJUTANT GENERAL 69

STATE OF NORTH CAROLINA
ADJUTANT GENERAL'S DEPARTMENT
RALEIGH

GENERAL ORDERS 2 July 1952
No.   15

So much of Par. 2c, G. O. No. 11, this Department, dated 10 June 1952, pertaining to certain NCNG units attending Field Training, Fort McClellan, Alabama, as reads, "Capt Melvin C. Holmes, 0-1822276, Hq Hq Btry 113th FA Bn, Franklinton, N. C.," is AMENDED to read, *"1st Lt Franklin P. Redmond, 0-976029, Hq Hq Btry 113th FA Bn, Franklinton, N. C."*

By Order of the Governor:

JOHN H. MANNING
Major General
The Adjutant General

OFFICIAL

WILLARD R. BLOXTON
Military Executive Officer
Adjutant General's Department

STATE OF NORTH CAROLINA
ADJUTANT GENERAL'S DEPARTMENT
RALEIGH

GENERAL ORDERS 14 July 1952
No.   16

So much of Par. 2c, G. O. No. 11, this Department, dated 10 June 1952, pertaining to certain NCNG units attending Field Training, Fort McClellan, Alabama, as reads, "Capt Shelton G. Scott, 0-1583642, Svc Co 119th Inf (Return to home station only), Fort McClellan, Alabama," is AMENDED to read, *"2nd Lt Benjamin C. Harrell, 0-999787, Svc Co 119th Inf (Return to home station only), Fort McClellan, Alabama."*

By Order of the Governor:

JOHN H. MANNING
Major General
The Adjutant General

OFFICIAL

WILLARD R. BLOXTON
Military Executive Officer
Adjutant General's Department

REPORT OF THE ADJUTANT GENERAL

STATE OF NORTH CAROLINA
ADJUTANT GENERAL'S DEPARTMENT
RALEIGH

GENERAL ORDERS   25 July 1952
No.   17

Par. 2, G. O. No. 14, AGD, NC, dtd 26 June 1952, is AMENDED to read as follows:

"The 8156th Air Base Squadron will be discontinued effective 9 July 1952 and personnel and equipment transferred to the 156th Fighter-Interceptor Squadron. The 156th Fighter-Interceptor Squadron is authorized to recruit its full strengths authorized under the above T/O's."

By Order of the Governor:

JOHN H. MANNING
Major General
The Adjutant General

OFFICIAL

WILLARD R. BLOXTON
Military Executive Officer
Adjutant General's Department

STATE OF NORTH CAROLINA
ADJUTANT GENERAL'S DEPARTMENT
RALEIGH

GENERAL ORDERS 11 August 1952
No. 18

1. With profound sorrow the death of CAPT DAVID FINLEY DAVIS, 0-1298644, Commanding Officer, Co. A, 120th Inf, NCNG, station Burlington, N. C. on 10 August 1952, is announced.

2. Capt Davis was born at Graham, N. C., 21 December 1919, and later in life moved to Burlington, N. C. At the time of his death, Capt Davis was associated with the Gates Construction Company at Graham, N. C.

3. Capt Davis was a young man of sterling qualities. He was admired by and had the confidence of those with whom he came in contact. In his sudden death, his community lost a valued citizen. The Armed Forces has lost a most valuable, efficient, and faithful officer.

4. RECORD OF MILITARY SERVICE.—Capt Davis served as an enlisted man, 120th Infantry, NCNG, during the period 27 February 1936—26 December 1937, 21 January 1938—15 September 1940, entering Active Military Service with the Med. Det., 120th Inf. on 16 September 1940, receiving an appointment as 2nd Lt, Inf, on 3 November 1942. After demonstration of his capabilities, Capt Davis was promoted to 1st Lt, Army of the United States, on 1 July 1944, and continued in the active Federal service in that grade until 31 October 1945. Upon release from the active Federal service, he remained on an inactive status in the Army of the United States until 19 January 1948, at which time he received an appointment as 1st Lt, Inf, NCNG, assigned Plat. Comdr., Co. A, 120th Inf, NCNG; however, during period 3 March 1947—1 January 1948, Capt Davis rendered service in the grade of T/Sgt., Co. A, 120th Inf, lending his support in the activation of that command. On 27 October 1948, Capt Davis was reassigned as Commanding Officer, Co. A, 120th Inf, receiving his promotion to the grade of Captain on 6 January 1950. Capt Davis was wounded four times with the 9th Infantry before his release in 1945 to Inactive duty status, after seeing action in Germany, Belgium, France, Africa, Sicily, and Holland. He was awarded the Silver Star and Bronze Star with one cluster for gallantry in action.

5. Next of kin.—Mrs. Betty Dixon Davis (Wife), Brookwood Garden Apt, Burlington, N. C.

By Order of the Governor:

JOHN H. MANNING
Major General
The Adjutant General

OFFICIAL
DAVID W. DONOVAN
Military Personnel Officer
Adjutant General's Department

REPORT OF THE ADJUTANT GENERAL

STATE OF NORTH CAROLINA
ADJUTANT GENERAL'S DEPARTMENT
RALEIGH

GENERAL ORDERS 9 September 1952
No. 19

Redesignation & Reorganization of 3624th Ordnance Medium Maintenance Co., NCNG

1. PAC Letter, NGB, NG-AROTO 325.4 General, Subject: "Redesignation and Reorganization of National Guard Nondivisional Ordnance Companies," dated 20 August 1952, the 3624th Ordnance Medium Maintenance Company, North Carolina National Guard, is hereby redesignated and reorganized in accordance with T/O&E indicated below, *effective 15 September 1952.* Maximum authorized strength for officers and warrant officers is listed in Column 7 and enlisted strength in Column 8 of appropriate T/O&E:

	T/O&E & Date		*Unit Structure*	
Old Designation	No.	Date	Orgn	Equip.
3624th Ordnance Medium Maintenance Co.				
New Designation				
3624th Ordnance Company (Direct Support)	9–7A	17 July 52	Column 7 Sec. II	Column 5 Sec. III

2. The provisions of NGB Circular No. 22, dated 24 September 1948, apply to this reorganization.

3. The number of grades for each MOS, as shown in column 16 through 21 inclusive (Section II (Organization)) of all tables are authorized provided the total enlisted strength does not exceed the total shown in column 8. Personnel rendered surplus by this reorganization will be governed by the provisions of paragraph 6, NGR 15 and paragraph 20, NGR 130.

4. Since the T/O&E referred to above includes a Section III (Equipment) and such section contains a full strength allowance column (column 4) and a reduced strength allowance column (column 5), National Guard Reduction Tables now being followed (for equipment only) will no longer be required nor be in effect on and after the date of reorganization.

By Order of the Governor:

JOHN H. MANNING
Major General
The Adjutant General

OFFICIAL
THOMAS B. LONGEST
Military Operations Officer
Adjutant General's Department

Report of The Adjutant General

STATE OF NORTH CAROLINA
ADJUTANT GENERAL'S DEPARTMENT
RALEIGH

GENERAL ORDERS
No. 20

9 September 1952

1. Pursuant to Sec. 93, National Defense Act, as amended, and the provisions of Air National Guard Regulations 123-1, 28 May 1952, Annual General Inspection of the following North Carolina Air National Guard unit will be conducted by officers of the Regular Air Force detailed by the Commanding General, Fourteenth Air Force, at the place and on the date indicated:

Unit	Location	Date
Hq, NC Air National Guard	Morris Field Charlotte NC	22 Sept 52

Inspector
Lt Col H. B. Eliker

2. All property, arms, clothing and equipment will be thoroughly cleaned and put in good condition. Property in supply rooms and individual lockers will be neatly and carefully arranged, in order that the inspecting officer may check their condition without a loss of time.

3. The inspection will be formal. The unit commander will review carefully ANGR 123-1; AFR 123-2 and present the unit for inspection according to the directives contained therein.

4. The expense enjoined is necessary in the military service.

By Order of the Governor:

JOHN H. MANNING
Major General
The Adjutant General

OFFICIAL
THOMAS B. LONGEST
Military Operations Officer
Adjutant General's Department

STATE OF NORTH CAROLINA
ADJUTANT GENERAL'S DEPARTMENT
RALEIGH

GENERAL ORDERS
No. 21

11 September 1952

Reorganization of 119th and 120th Infantry Regiments, NCNG

1. PAC Letter, NGB, NG-AROTO 325.4 General, Subject: "Reorganization of National Guard Infantry Regiments," dated 28 August 1952, the 119th and 120th Infantry Regiments, North Carolina National Guard, are hereby reorganized in accordance with T/O&Es indicated below, *effective 1 October 1952*. Maximum authorized strength for officers and warrant officers is listed in Column 7 and enlisted strength in Column 8 of appropriate T/O&Es:

74   REPORT OF THE ADJUTANT GENERAL

	T/O&E & Date		Unit Structure	
Unit	No.	Date	Orgn	Equip
119th Infantry	7–11	15 May 52	Column 7 Sec. II	Column 5 Sec. III
Hq. & Hq. Co., 119th Infantry	7–12	15 May 52	Column 7 Sec. II	Column 5 Sec. III
Service Company, 119th Infantry	7–13	15 May 52	Column 7 Sec. II	Column 5 Sec. III
Heavy Mortar Co., 119th Inf.	7–14	15 May 52	Column 7 Sec. II	Column 5 Sec. III
Tank Co., 119th Inf. (90mm Gun)	17–37	15 May 52	Column 7 Sec. II	Column 5 Sec. III
Medical Company, 119th Inf.	8–7	15 May 52	Column 7 Sec. II	Column 5 Sec. III
1st Battalion, 119th Infantry	7–15	15 May 52	Column 7 Sec. II	Column 5 Sec. III
Hq. & Hq. Co., 1st Bn., 119th Inf.	7–16	15 May 52	Column 7 Sec. II	Column 5 Sec. III
Company A, 119th Infantry	7–17	15 May 52	Column 7 Sec. II	Column 5 Sec. III
Company B, 119th Infantry	7–17	15 May 52	Column 7 Sec. II	Column 5 Sec. III
Company C, 119th Infantry	7–17	15 May 52	Column 7 Sec. II	Column 5 Sec. III
Company D, 119th Infantry	7–18	15 May 52	Column 7 Sec. II	Column 5 Sec. III
2nd Battalion, 119th Infantry	7–15	15 May 52	Column 7 Sec. II	Column 5 Sec. III
Hq. & Hq. Co., 2nd Bn., 119th Inf.	7–16	15 May 52	Column 7 Sec. II	Column 5 Sec. III
Company E, 119th Infantry	7–17	15 May 52	Column 7 Sec. II	Column 5 Sec. III
Company F, 119th Infantry	7–17	15 May 52	Column 7 Sec. II	Column 5 Sec. III
Company G, 119th Infantry	7–17	15 May 52	Column 7 Sec. II	Column 5 Sec. III
Company H, 119th Infantry	7–18	15 May 52	Column 7 Sec. II	Column 5 Sec. III
3rd Battalion, 119th Infantry	7–15	15 May 52	Column 7 Sec. II	Column 5 Sec. III
Hq. & Hq. Co., 3rd Bn., 119th Inf.	7–16	15 May 52	Column 7 Sec. II	Column 5 Sec. III
Company I, 119th Infantry	7–17	15 May 52	Column 7 Sec. II	Column 5 Sec. III
Company K, 119th Infantry	7–17	15 May 52	Column 7 Sec. II	Column 5 Sec. III
Company L, 119th Infantry	7–17	15 May 52	Column 7 Sec. II	Column 5 Sec. III
Company M, 119th Infantry	7–18	15 May 52	Column 7 Sec. II	Column 5 Sec. III
120th Infantry	7–11	15 May 52	Column 7 Sec. II	Column 5 Sec. III
Hq. & Hq. Company, 120th Infantry	7–12	15 May 52	Column 7 Sec. II	Column 5 Sec. III

REPORT OF THE ADJUTANT GENERAL

Unit	T/O&E & Date		Unit Structure	
	No.	Date	Orgn	Equip.
Service Company, 120th Infantry	7-13	15 May 52	Column 7 Sec. II	Column 5 Sec. III
Heavy Mortar Company, 120th Inf.	7-14	15 May 52	Column 7 Sec. II	Column 5 Sec. III
Tank Co., 120th Inf. (90mm Gun)	17-37	15 May 52	Column Sec. II	Column 5 Sec. III
Medical Company, 120th Infantry	8-7	15 May 52	Column 7 Sec. II	Column 5 Sec. III
1st Battalion, 120th Infantry	7-15	15 May 52	Column 7 Sec. II	Column 5 Sec. III
Hq. & Hq. Co., 1st Bn., 120th Inf.	7-16	15 Ma5 y2	Column 7 Sec. II	Column 5 Sec. III
Company A, 120th Infantry	7-17	15 May 52	Column 7 Sec. II	Column 5 Sec. III
Company B, 120th Infantry	7-17	15 May 52	Column 7 Sec. II	Column 5 Sec. III
Company C, 120th Infantry	7-17	15 May 52	Column 7 Sec. II	Column 5 Sec. III
Company D, 120th Infantry	7-18	15 May 52	Column 7 Sec. II	Column 5 Sec. III
2nd Battalion, 120th Infantry	7-15	15 May 52	Column 7 Sec. II	Column 5 Sec. III
Hq. & Hq. Co., 2nd Bn., 120th Inf.	7-16	15 May 52	Column 7 Sec. II	Column 5 Sec. III
Company E, 120th Infantry	7-17	15 May 52	Column 7 Sec. II	Column 5 Sec. III
Company F, 120th Infantry	7-17	15 May 52	Column 7 Sec. II	Column 5 Sec. III
Company G, 120th Infantry	7-17	15 May 52	Column 7 Sec. II	Column 5 Sce. III
Company H, 120th Infantry	7-18	15 May 52	Column 7 Sec. II	Column 5 Sec. III
3rd Battalion, 120th Infantry	7-15	15 May 52	Column 7 Sec. II	Column 5 Sec. III
Hq. & Hq. Co., 3rd Bn., 120th Inf.	7-16	15 May 52	Column 7 Sec. II	Column 5 Sec. III
Company I, 120th Infantry	7-17	15 May 52	Column 7 Sec. II	Column 5 Sec. III
Company K, 120th Infantry	7-17	15 May 52	Column 7 Sec. II	Column 5 Sec. III
Company L, 120th Infantry	7-17	15 May 52	Column 7 Sec. II	Column 5 Sec. III
Company M, 120th Infantry	7-18	15 May 52	Column 7 Sec. II	Column 5 Sec. III

2. The provisions of NGB Circular No. 22, dated 24 September 1948, apply to this reorganization.

3. The number of grades for each MOS, as shown in column 16 through 21, inclusive (Section II (Organization)) of all tables are authorized provided the total enlisted strength does not exceed the total shown in column 8. Personnel rendered surplus by this reorganization will be governed by the provisions of paragraph 6, NGR 15 and paragraph 20, NGR 130.

Report of the Adjutant General

4. Since the T/O&Es referred to above include a Section III (Equipment) and such Section contains a full strength allowance column (column 4) and a reduced strength allowance column (column 5), National Guard Reduction Tables now being followed (for equipment only) will no longer be required nor be in effect on and after the date of reorganization.

By Order of the Governor:

OFFICIAL
THOMAS B. LONGEST
Military Operations Officer
Adjutant General's Department

JOHN H. MANNING
Major General
The Adjutant General

STATE OF NORTH CAROLINA
ADJUTANT GENERAL'S DEPARTMENT
RALEIGH

GENERAL ORDERS
No. 22

12 September 1952

1. Purusant to Sec. 93, National Defense Act, as amended, and the provisions of Sec. II, National Guard Regulations 48, 30 October 1950, Annual Armory Inspections of the following North Carolina National Guard units will be conducted by officers of the Regular Army detailed by the Commanding General, Third Army, at the places and on the dates indicated:

Unit	Location	Date	Inspector
Btry. B, 112th FA Bn.	Spindale	15 Sep. 52	Lt. Col. R. O. Nunamaker
Btry. A, 112th FA Bn.	Forest City	16 Sep. 52	Lt. Col. R. O. Nunamaker
Hq. Hq. Btry., 112th FA Bn.	Lenoir	17 Sep. 52	Lt. Col. R. O. Nunamaker
Hq. Hq. Btry. (Pt), 30th Div. Arty.	Lenoir	17 Sep. 52	Lt. Col. R. O. Nunamaker
Svc. Btry., 112th FA Bn.	Lenoir	18 Sep. 52	Lt. Col. R. O. Nunamaker
Hq. Hq. Btry, 130th AAA AW Bn.	Red Springs	22 Sep. 52	Lt. Col. C. B. Irwin
Btry. B, 130th AAA AW Bn.	St Pauls	23 Sep. 52	Lt. Col. C. B. Irwin
Mdm. Tk. Co., 119th Inf.	Parkton	24 Sep. 52	Lt. Col. C. B. Irwin
Btry. A, 130th AAA AW Bn.	Raeford	29 Sep. 52	Lt. Col. C. B. Irwin
Hq. Hq. Co., 1st Bn. 119th Inf.	Durham	29 Sep. 52	Lt. Col. R. O. Nunamaker
Btry. C, 130th AAA AW Bn.	Sanford	30 Sep. 52	Lt. Col. C. B. Irwin
Hq. Hq. Co., 119th Inf.	Durham	30 Sep. 52	Lt. Col. R. O. Nunamaker
Btry. D, 130th AAA AW Bn.	Southern Pines	1 Oct. 52	Lt. Col. C. B. Irwin
Co. D, 119th Inf.	Durham	1 Oct. 52	Lt. Col. R. O. Nunamaker
Btry. A, 725th AAA AW Bn.	Shallotte	6 Oct. 52	Maj. E. W. Buchanan
Co. H, 120th Inf.	Hickory	6 Oct. 52	Lt. Col. C. B. Irwin
Hq. Hq. Co., 167th MP Bn.	Ahoskie	6 Oct. 52	Lt. Col. J. W. Levy
Btry. C, 113th FA Bn.	Roxboro	6 Oct. 52	Lt. Col. R. O. Nunamaker
Med. Det., 505th FA Bn.	Greensboro	6 Oct. 52	Lt. Col. P. J. Brown
123d SRMU	Wilmington	7 Oct. 52	Maj E. W. Buchanan
Hq. Hq. Btry., 252d AAA Gp.	Wilmington	7 Oct. 52	Maj. E. W. Buchanan
Co. G, 120th Inf.	Salisbury	7 Oct. 52	Lt. Col. C. B. Irwin
Co. E, 119th Inf.	Roanoke Rapids	7 Oct. 52	Lt. Col. J. W. Levy
Co. C, 119th Inf.	Henderson	7 Oct. 52	Lt. Col. R. O. Nunamaker
Svc. Btry, 505th FA Bn.	Greensboro	7 Oct. 52	Lt. Col. P. J. Brown
Svc Co., 119th Inf.	Elizabeth City	8 Oct. 52	Lt. Col. J. W. Levy
Co. I, 119th Inf.	Wilmington	8 Oct. 52	Maj. E. W. Buchanan

Unit	Location	Date	Inspector
Hq. Hq. Co., 2d Bn., 120th Inf.	Asheboro	8 Oct. 52	Lt. Col. C. B. Irwin
Co. B, 119th Inf.	Warrenton	8 Oct. 52	Lt. Col. R. O. Nunamaker
Btry. A, 505th FA Bn.	Greensboro	8 Oct. 52	Lt. Col. P. J. Brown
Co. A, 167th MP Bn.	Windsor	9 Oct. 52	Lt. Col. J. W. Levy
Btry. C, 725th AAA AW Bn.	Bladenboro	9 Oct. 52	Maj. E. W. Buchanan
3624th Ord. M. Co.	Butner	9 Oct. 52	Lt. Col. C. B. Irwin
Hq. Hq. Btry., 113th FA Bn.	Louisburg	9 Oct. 52	Lt. Col. R. O. Nunamaker
Btry. B, 505th FA Bn.	Greensboro	9 Oct. 52	Lt. Col. P. J. Brown
Svc. Btry., 113th FA Bn.	Youngsville	10 Oct. 52	Lt. Col. R. O. Nunamaker
Btry. C, 505th FA Bn.	Greensboro	10 Oct. 52	Lt. Col. P. J. Brown
Hq. Hq. Btry., IV Corps Arty.	Charlotte	13 Oct. 52	Lt. Col. R. E. McMurray
Hq. Hq. Co., 3d Bn., 119th Inf.	Clinton	13 Oct. 52	Maj. E. W. Buchanan
Co., F, 119th Inf.	Tarboro	13 Oct. 52	Lt. Col. J. W. Levy
Co. A, 119th Inf.	Oxford	13 Oct. 52	Lt. Col. R. O. Nunamaker
217th AAA Det. (RCAT)	Raleigh	13 Oct. 52	Lt. Col. C. B. Irwin
94th Army Band	Raleigh	13 Oct. 52	Lt. Col. C. B. Irwin
Hq. Hq. Co., 2d Bn., 119th Inf.	Wilson	14 Oct. 52	Lt. Col. J. W. Levy
Hq. (Pt), 30th Inf. Div.	Raleigh	14 Oct. 52	Lt. Col. C. B. Irwin
121st AAA Opns. Det.	Charlotte	14 Oct. 52	Lt. Col. R. E. McMurray
Btry. B, 725th AAA AW Bn.	Fair Bluff	14 Oct. 52	Maj. E. W. Buchanan
Btry. A, 113th FA Bn.	Zebulon	14 Oct. 52	Lt. Col. R. O. Nunamaker
Hq. Hq. Co., 120th Inf.	Reidsville	14 Oct. 52	Lt . Col. P. J. Brown
Hq. Hq. Co., 3d Bn., 120th Inf.	Kings Mtn	15 Oct. 52	Lt. Col. R. E. McMurray
Hq. Hq. Btry., 725th AAA AW Bn.	Whiteville	15 Oct. 52	Maj. E. W. Buchanan
Med. Det., 30th Inf. Div.	Apex	15 Oct. 52	Lt. Col. C. B. Irwin
Hq. Co., 30th Inf. Div.	Apex	15 Oct. 52	Lt. Col. C. B. Irwin
Co. B, 167th MP Bn.	Lasker	15 Oct. 52	Lt. Col. J. W. Levy
Btry. B, 113th FA Bn.	Dunn	15 Oct. 52	Lt. Col. R. O. Nunamaker
Co. A, 120th Inf.	Burlington	15 Oct. 52	Lt. Col. P. J. Brown
Co. H, 119th Inf.	Scotland Neck	16 Oct. 52	Lt. Col. J. W. Levy
Co. L, 119th Inf.	Goldsboro	16 Oct. 52	Maj E. W. Buchanan
Co. K, 120th Inf.	Gastonia	16 Oct. 52	Lt. Col. R. E. McMurray
Co. K, 119th Inf	Fayetteville	20 Oct. 52	Maj. E. W. Buchanan
Med Co., 120th Inf.	Mocksville	20 Oct. 52	Lt. Col. C. B. Irwin
Med. Co., 119th Inf.	Wilson	20 Oct. 52	Lt. Col. J. W. Levy
Co. M, 120th Inf.	Shelby	20 Oct. 52	Lt. Col. R. O. Nunamaker
Co. B, 120th Inf.	Winston-Salem	20 Oct. 52	Lt. Col. P. J. Brown
Btry. D, 725th AAA AW Bn.	Benson	21 Oct. 52	Maj. E. W. Buchanan
Co. E, 120th Inf.	Concord	21 Oct. 52	Lt. Col. C. B. Irwin
Co. G, 119th Inf.	Rocky Mount	21 Oct. 52	Lt. Col. J. W. Levy
Co. I, 120th Inf.	Newton	21 Oct. 52	Lt. Col. R. O. Nunamaker
Co. D, 120th Inf.	Winston Salem	21 Oct. 52	Lt. Col. P. J. Brown
Hq. Hq. Btry., 196th FA Gp.	Kinston	22 Oct. 52	Maj. E. W. Buchanan
Co. F, 120th Inf.	Albemarle	22 Oct. 52	Lt. Col. C. B. Irwin
Hv. Mtr. Co., 119th Inf	Edenton	22 Oct. 52	Lt. Col. J. W Levy
Co. L, 120th Inf.	Morganton	22 Oct. 52	Lt. Col. R. O. Nunamaker
Co. C, 120th Inf.	Lexington	22 Oct. 52	Lt. Col. P. J. Brown
Co. M, 119th Inf.	Warsaw	23 Oct. 52	Maj. E. W. Buchanan
Hq. Hq. Co., 1st Bn., 120th Inf.	Mt. Airy	27 Oct. 52	Lt. Col. P. J. Brown
Svc Co., 120th Inf.	Asheville	28 Oct. 52	Lt. Col. R. E. McMurray
Btry. C, 112th FA Bn.	N. Wilkesboro	28 Oct. 52	Lt. Col. P. J. Brown
30th Sig. Co.	Canton	29 Oct. 52	Lt. Col. R. E. McMurray
Hv. Mtr. Co., 120th Inf.	Leaksville	29 Oct. 52	Lt. Col. P. J. Brown
Mdm. Tk. Co., 120th Inf.	Waynesville	30 Oct. 52	Lt. Col. R. E. McMurray

2. Armory Inspections will be made in two (2) parts: an administrative inspection of armory facilities, property, official records, and general administration. The organization commander, first sergeant, caretaker, supply sergeant and administrative assistant will be present at the armory at the

time designated for the administrative inspection. There will also be an inspection of the state of training of all personnel of the organization and the adequacy of equipment. The time devoted to the training inspection should not exceed the time required in a normal armory drill period. The hours of these two parts of the inspection will be set by arrangement between the unit commander and the inspecting officer.

3. All property, arms, clothing and equipment will be thoroughly cleaned and put in good condition. Property in supply rooms and individual lockers will be neatly and carefully arranged, in order that the inspecting officer may check their condition without loss of time.

4. The inspection will be formal. Unit commanders will review carefully Sec. II, NGR 48; SR 20-10-8, 21 July 1949, as amended, and present the unit for inspection according to directives contained therein.

By Order of the Governor:

JOHN H. MANNING
Major General
The Adjutant General

OFFICIAL
THOMAS B. LONGEST
Military Operations Officer
Adjutant General's Department

STATE OF NORTH CAROLINA
ADJUTANT GENERAL'S DEPARTMENT
RALEIGH

GENERAL ORDERS
No. 23

16 September 1952

Redesignation of Tank Companies of Infantry Regiments

PAC Letter, NGB, NG-AROTO 325.4 General, Subject: "Reorganization of National Guard Infantry Regiments," dated 10 September 1952, the following units, North Carolina National Guard, are hereby redesignated in accordance with T/O&Es as indicated below, *effective 1 October 1952.*

Old Designation	T/O&E & Date		Unit Structure	
	No.	Date	Orgn	Equip.
Tank Co. (Medium), 119th Inf. Regt.				
Tank Co. (Mediun), 120th Inf. Regt.				
New Designation				
Tank Co., 119th Inf. Regt. (90mm Gun)	17-37	15 May 52	Column 7 Sec. II	Column 5 Sec III
Tank Co., 120th Inf. Regt. (90mm Gun)	17-37	15 May 52	Column 7 Sec. II	Column 5 Sec. III

By Order of the Governor:

JOHN H. MANNING
Major General
The Adjutant General

OFFICIAL
THOMAS B. LONGEST
Military Operations Officer
Adjutant General's Department

Report of The Adjutant General

STATE OF NORTH CAROLINA
ADJUTANT GENERAL'S DEPARTMENT
RALEIGH

GENERAL ORDERS 19 September 1952
No. 24

1. Pursuant to Sec. 93, National Defense Act, as amended, and the provisions of Sec. II, National Guard Regulations 48, 30 December 1950, Annual Armory Inspections of the following North Carolina National Guard units will be conducted by officers of the Regular Army detailed by the Commanding General, Third Army, at the places and on the dates indicated:

Unit	Location	Date	Inspector
Hq. Hq. Btry., 505th FA Bn.	Greensboro	13 Oct. 52	Lt. Col. P. J. Brown
Hq. Hq. Btry., 252nd FA Gp.	Greensboro	6 Oct. 52	Lt. Col. P. J. Brown

2. Armory Inspections will be made in two (2) parts: an administrative inspection of armory facilities, property, official records, and general administration. The organization commander, first sergeant, caretaker, supply sergeant and administrative assistant will be present at the armory at the time designated for the administrative inspection. There will also be an inspection of the state of training of all personnel of the organization and the adequacy of equipment. The time devoted to the training inspection should not exceed the time required in a normal armory drill period. The hours of these two parts of the inspection will be set by arrangement between the unit commander and the inspecting officer.

3. All property, arms, clothing and equipment will be thoroughly cleaned and put in good condition. Property in supply rooms and individual lockers will be neatly and carefully arranged, in order that the inspecting officers may check their condition without loss of time.

4. The inspection will be formal. Unit commanders will review carefully Sec. II, NGR 48; SR 20-10-8, 21 July 1949, as amended, and present the unit for inspection according to directives contained therein.

By Order of the Governor:

JOHN H. MANNING
Major General
The Adjutant General

OFFICIAL
THOMAS B. LONGEST
Military Operations Officer
Adjutant General's Department

STATE OF NORTH CAROLINA
ADJUTANT GENERAL'S DEPARTMENT
RALEIGH

GENERAL ORDERS 30 September 1952
No. 25

So much of Par. 1, G.O. No. 22, this Department, dated 12 September 1952, as pertains to the following units, NCNG, is RESCINDED and the following substituted in lieu thereof:

REPORT OF THE ADJUTANT GENERAL

Unit	Location	Date	Inspector
Co. G, 120th Inf.	Salisbury, N. C.	6 Oct. 52	Lt. Col. C. B. Irwin
Co. H, 120th Inf.	Hickory, N. C.	7 Oct. 52	Lt. Col. C. B. Irwin
Co. L, 119th Inf.	Goldsboro, N. C.	14 Oct. 52	Lt. Col. C. B. Irwin
Hq. (Pt), 30th Inf Div.	Raleigh, N. C.	21 Oct. 52	Col. J. D. Salmon

By Order of the Governor:

OFFICIAL
THOMAS B. LONGEST
Military Operations Officer
Adjutant General's Department

JOHN H. MANNING
Major General
The Adjutant General

STATE OF NORTH CAROLINA
ADJUTANT GENERAL'S DEPARTMENT
RALEIGH

GENERAL ORDERS   7 October 1952
No.   26

1. PAC Ltr, Departments of the Army and the Air Force, National Guard Bureau, file NG AFOTP, Subject: "'Authority to Activate," dated 30 September 1952, the activation of the 263rd Communications Squadron, Operations NCANG, is hereby announced, effective 8 October 1952.

2. The 263rd Communications Squadron, Operations NCANG, will be organized in accordance with T/O and station assignments as listed below:

WADESBORO, N. C.

T/O	Date	Composition	Authorized Strength		
			Off	Amn	Agg
1-2233	1 Jan. 52	1 x Parts IIB, IIN, IIV, IIAL, IIAP, IIT, IIG; 3 x Parts IIZ	6	59	65

BADIN, N. C.

T/O	Date	Composition	Authorized Strength		
			Off	Amn	Agg
1-2233	1 Jan. 52	1 x Parts IIN, IIV, IIAL, IIAP, IIT, IIG, IIZ	2	34	36

3. The Squadron will be presented for inspection for federal recognition according to the procedures contained in ANGR 20-38, dated 31 May 1951, and minimum strength for federal recognition and for maintaining continued

federal recognition will be as listed in strength table attachment to ANGL 35-01A, dated 11 August 1952.

By Order of the Governor:

OFFICIAL
WILLARD R. BLOXTON
Military Executive Officer
Adjutant General's Department

JOHN H. MANNING
Major General
The Adjutant General

STATE OF NORTH CAROLINA
ADJUTANT GENERAL'S DEPARTMENT
RALEIGH

GENERAL ORDERS
No. 27

15 October 1952

SECTION I

Organization of NGUS Units, NCNG

1. Pursuant to authority, National Guard Bureau, NGB Form 5, 6 Oct 52, the following units North Carolina National Guard are organized effective 3 November 1952 as National Guard Units under Public Law 461, 82nd Congress, under T/O&Es, home station and strength requirements as indicated:

Unit Designation	Applicable T/O & E	Maximum Authorized Strength		Required for Federal Recognition	
		Off & WO	EM	Off & WO	EM
Hq. & Hq. Btry., 540th Field Artillery Batallion (NGUS) Station: High Point, N. C.	6-416 18 July 50 w/Cl & 2	8	28	2	3
Battery A, 540th Field Artillery Battalion (NGUS) Station: High Point, N. C.	6-417 18 July 50 w/Cl & 2	3	33	1	3

2. Units will be presented for inspection for federal recognition in accordance with procedures contained in Section III, NGR 15, dated 25 June 1948. Inspecting Officer to be designated by Commanding General, Third Army, Fort McPherson, Georgia.

3. The following records will be prepared and presented to the Inspecting Officer:

    a. Copy of NGB Form 5, authority to organize the unit, and applicable T/O&E from the Chief, NGB, to The Adjutant General of North Carolina. Five (5) copies.

    b. Initial roster of unit WD NGB Form 100. Five (5) copies.

REPORT OF THE ADJUTANT GENERAL

    c. Special Orders assigning individual officers to the unit and duties therein. Five (5) copies.

    d. Enlistment record WD NGB Form 21 for each member executed in three (3) copies to be completed.

    e. Service Record, NGB Form 24, for each member to be completed to date.

SECTION II

Attachment of Unit

Pursuant to authority contained in Par. 7.1, Changes No. 2 to NGR 15, 15 May 1952, the 540th FA Battalion (NGUS) North Carolina National Guard, is attached to 252nd FA Group, North Carolina National Guard, effective 3 November 1952.

By Order of the Governor:

OFFICIAL
THOMAS B. LONGEST
Military Operations Officer
Adjutant General's Department

JOHN H. MANNING
Major General
The Adjutant General

STATE OF NORTH CAROLINA
ADJUTANT GENERAL'S DEPARTMENT
RALEIGH

GENERAL ORDERS   10 November 1952
No.   28

SECTION I

Organization of Unit, NCNG

1. Pursuant to authority contained in NGB Form 5, National Guard Bureau, 28 October 1952, the following unit, North Carolina National Guard, is organized under T/O&E, home station and strength requirements as indicated effective 18 November 1952:

Unit Designation	Applicable T/O & E	Maximum Authorized Strength		Required for Federal Recognition	
		Off	EM	Off	EM
Separate Detachment Headquarters Company 30th Inf. Div. (Light Aviation Section) Station: Raleigh-Durham Airport, North Carolina	7-2N 7 July 48 w/Change 1 and Par 13, Change 2	8	16	2	2

2. Unit will be presented for inspection for federal recognition in accordance with procedures contained in Section III, NGR 15, dated 25 June 1948. Inspecting Officer to be designated by Commanding General, Third Army, Fort McPherson, Georgia.

REPORT OF THE ADJUTANT GENERAL

3. The following records will be prepared and presented to the Inspecting Officer:

   a. Copy of NGB Form 5, authority to organize the unit, and applicable T/O&E from the Chief, NGB, to The Adjutant General of North Carolina. Five (5) copies.
   b. Initial roster of unit WD NGB Form 100. Five (5) copies.
   c. Special Orders assigning officers and enlisted men to the unit and duties therein. Five (5) copies.
   d. Enlistment record WD NGB Form 21 for each member executed in three (3) copies to be completed.
   e. Service Record, NGB Form 24, for each member to be completed to date.

SECTION II

Redesignation of Unit, NCNG

1. Pursuant to authority contained in letter NG-AROTO 325.4—N. C., National Guard Bureau, 29 October 1952, subject, "Redesignation of National Guard Unit," the following federally recognized North Carolina National Guard unit is redesignated as indicated, effective 18 November 1952:

Old Designation	New Designation	Station	Effective Date of F/R
Headquarters Company 30th Infantry Division	Headquarters Company, 30th Infantry Div. (Less Sep. Det.)	Apex, N. C.	22 March 1948

By Order of the Governor:

JOHN H. MANNING
Major General
The Adjutant General

OFFICIAL
THOMAS B. LONGEST
Military Operations Officer
Adjutant General's Department

STATE OF NORTH CAROLINA
ADJUTANT GENERAL'S DEPARTMENT
RALEIGH

GENERAL ORDERS   12 November 1952
No.   29

Organization of NGUS Units, NCNG

1. Pursuant to authority, National Guard Bureau, NGB Form 5, 2 Sept 52, the following units North Carolina National Guard are organized effective 12 November 1952 as National Guard Units under Public Law 461, 82nd Congress, under T/O&Es, home station and strength requirements as indicated:

Report of the Adjutant General

Unit Designation	Applicable T/O & E	Maximum Authorized Strength		Required for Federal Recognition	
		Off & WO	EM	Off & WO	EM
Hq. Hq. & Svc. Company, 378th Engineer Combat Bn. (NGUS) Station: Charlotte, N. C.	5-36 15 Sep. 48 w/C1 & 2 RT 5-36-22 1 May 49	10	39	3	4
Company A, 378th Engineer Combat Battalion (NGUS) Station: Lincolnton, N. C.	5-37 15 Sep. 48 w/C1 & 2 RT 5-37-22 1 May 49	3	43	1	5
Company B, 378th Engineer Combat Battalion (NGUS) Station: Charlotte, N. C.	5-37 15 Sep. 48 w/C1 & 2 RT 5-37-22 1 May 49	3	43	1	5
Company C, 378th Engineer Combat Battalion ⁵NGUS⁴ Station: Statesville, N. C.	5-37 15 Sep 48 w/C1 &2 RT 5-37-22 1 May 49	3	43	1	5

2. Units will be presented for inspection for federal recognition in accordance with procedures contained in Section III, NGR 15, dated 25 June 1948. Inspecting Officer to be designated by Commanding General, Third Army, Fort McPherson, Georgia.

3. The following records will be prepared and presented to the Inspecting Officer:

    a. Copy of NGB Form 5, authority to organize the unit, and applicable T/O&E from the Chief, NGB, to The Adjutant General of North Carolina. Five (5) copies.

    b. Initial roster of unit WD NGB Form 100. Five (5) copies.

    c. Special Orders assigning officers and enlisted men to the unit and duties therein. Five (5) copies.

    d. Enlistment record WD NGB Form 21 for each member executed in three (3) copies for new enlistees and one (1) copy for EM with current service obligation.

    e. Service Record, NGB Form 24, for each member to be completed to date.

By Order of the Governor:

OFFICIAL
THOMAS B. LONGEST
Military Operations Officer
Adjutant General's Department

JOHN H. MANNING
Major General
The Adjutant General

REPORT OF THE ADJUTANT GENERAL 85

STATE OF NORTH CAROLINA
ADJUTANT GENERAL'S DEPARTMENT
RALEIGH

GENERAL ORDERS 1 December 1952
No. 30

Redesignation of NC ANG Unit

Pursuant to authority contained in letter, Departments of the Army and Air Force, National Guard Bureau, file NG-AFOTP, subject: "Mission Assignment," dated 21 November 1952, the 156th Fighter Interceptor Squadron is redesignated the 156th Fighter Bomber Squadron, effective 1 December 1952.

By Order of the Governor:

JOHN H. MANNING
OFFICIAL *Major General*
WILLARD R. BLOXTON *The Adjutant General*
Military Executive Officer
Adjutant General's Department

STATE OF NORTH CAROLINA
ADJUTANT GENERAL'S DEPARTMENT
RALEIGH

GENERAL ORDERS 1 December 1952
No. 31

Reorganization of State Hq and Hq Detch NCNG

1. Pursuant to authority contained in letter, National Guard Bureau, NG-AROTO 325.4—N. C. (10 Nov 52), Subject: "Table of Organization, State Headquarters and Headquarters Detachment," dated 18 November 1952, the State Headquarters and Headquarters Detachment, North Carolina National Guard, is reorganized in accordance with the following Table of Organization, effective 10 November 1952:

Line	Grade	National Guard Section	Selective Service Section	Total
1	Maj. Gen.			
2	Brig. Gen.	1		1
3	Colonel	2	2	4
4	Lt. Colonel	4	4	8
5	Major	2	7	9
6	Captain	3	2	5
7	1st Lt.	1		1
8	Total Commissioned	13	15	28
9	WO		1	1
10	M/Sgt.	2		2
11	Sgt. 1st Cl.	3		3
12	Sgt.	4		4
13	Cpl.	5		5
14	Pfc.	13		13
15	Pvt.			
16	Total Enlisted	27		27
17	Aggregate	40	16	56

2. Personnel rendered surplus by this reorganization will be governed by the provisions of paragraph 6, NGR 15.

3. This Table of Organization supersedes previous Table of Organization contained in Section II, General Orders No. 36, this Department, dated 26 Nov. 51.

By Order of the Governor:

OFFICIAL
THOMAS B. LONGEST
Military Operations Officer
Adjutant General's Department

JOHN H. MANNING
Major General
The Adjutant General

STATE OF NORTH CAROLINA
ADJUTANT GENERAL'S DEPARTMENT
RALEIGH

GENERAL ORDERS
No. 32

2 December 1952

Reorganization of 30th Infantry Division Units NCNG

1. Pursuant to authority contained in letter, National Guard Bureau, NG-AROTO 325.4, General, Subject: "Reorganization of National Guard Infantry Division Units," dated 19 November 1952, the following units of the 30th Infantry Division, North Carolina National Guard, are hereby reorganized in accordance with T/O&Es indicated below, *effective 1 January 1953*. Maximum authorized strength for officers and warrant officers is listed in Column 7 and enlisted strength in Column 8 of appropriate T/O&Es:

Unit	T/O&E & Date		Unit Structure	
	No.	Date	Orgn	Equip.
Headquarters, 30th Infantry Division (In Part)	7-1	15 May 52	Column 7 Sec. II	Column 5 Sec. III
Headquarters Company 30th Infantry Div. (Less separate detachment)	7-2	15 May 52	Column 7 Sec. II	Column 5 Sec. III
Separate Detachment Headquarters Company 30th Infantry Division (Light Aviation Section)	7-2	15 May 52	Column 7 Sec. II Page 6	Column 5 Sec. III Page 13
Medical Detachment, Division Headquarters, 30th Infantry Div.	7-2	15 May 52	Column 7 Sec. II Page 8	Column 5 Sec. III Page 16
30th Signal Company (Infantry Division)	11-7	15 May 52	Column 7 Sec. II	Column 5 Sec. III

2. The provisions of NGB Circular No. 22, dated 24 September 1948, apply to this reorganization.

3. The number of grades for each MOS, as shown in columns 16 through 21, inclusive (Section II, Organization), are authorized provided the total

enlisted strength does not exceed the total shown in column 8. Personnel rendered surplus by this reorganization will be governed by the provisions of paragraph 6, NGR 15 and paragraph 20, NGR 130.

4. Since the T/O&Es referred to above include a Section III (Equipment) and such Section contains a full strength allowance column (column 4) and a reduced strength allowance column (column 5), National Guard Reduction Tables now being followed (for equipment only) will no longer be required nor be in effect on and after the date of reorganization.

By Order of the Governor:

OFFICIAL
THOMAS B. LONGEST
Military Operations Officer
Adjutant General's Department

JOHN H. MANNING
Major General
The Adjutant General

STATE OF NORTH CAROLINA
ADJUTANT GENERAL'S DEPARTMENT
RALEIGH

GENERAL ORDERS
No. 33

10 December 1952

Reorganization of 30th Infantry Division Artillery Units, NCNG

1. Pursuant to authority contained in letter, National Guard Bureau, NG-AROTO 325.4, General, Subject: "Reorganization of National Guard Division Artillery, Infantry Division," dated 26 November 1952, the following units of the 30th Infantry Division, North Carolina National Guard, are hereby reorganized in accordance with T/O&Es indicated below, *effective 1 January 1953*. Maximum authorized strength for officers and warrant officers is listed in Column 7 and enlisted strength in Column 8 of appropriate T/O&Es:

Unit	T/O&E & Date		Unit Structure	
	No.	Date	Orgn	Equip.
Hq. Hq. Battery, 30th Division Artillery (In Part)	6–101A	15 May 52	Column 7 Sec. II	Column 5 Sec. III
113th Field Artillery Battalion	6–125 w/Cl	15 May 52	Column 7 Sec. II Page 6	Column 5 Sec. III Page 13
Hq. Hq. Battery, 113th Field Artillery Battalion	6–126	15 May 52	Column 7 Sec. II Page 6	Column 5 Sec. III Page 15
Battery A, 113th Field Artillery Battalion	6–127	15 May 52	Column 7 Sec. II Page 5	Column 5 Sec. III Page 10
Battery B, 113th Field Artillery Battalion	6–127	15 May 52	Column 7 Sec. II Page 5	Column 5 Sec. III Page 10

Unit	T/O&E & Date		Unit Structure	
	No.	Date	Orgn	Equip.
Battery C, 113th Field Artillery Battalion	6-127	15 May 52	Column 7 Sec. II Page 5	Column 5 Sec. III Page 10
Service Battery, 113th Field Artillery Battalion	6-129	15 May 52	Column 7 Sec. II	Column 5 Sec. III
112th Field Artillery Battalion	6-125 w/Cl	15 May 52	Column 7 Sec. II Page 6	Column 5 Sec. III Page 13
Hq. Hq. Battery, 112th Field Artillery Battalion	6-126	15 May 52	Column 7 Sec. II Page 6	Co.umn 5 Sec. III Page 15
Battery A, 112th Field Artillery Batallion	6-127	15 May 52	Column 7 Sec. II Page 5	Column 5 Sec. III Page 10
Battery B, 112th Field Artillery Battalion	6-127	15 May 52	Column 7 Sec. II Page 5	Column 5 Sec. III Page 10
Battery C, 112th Field Artillery Battalion	6-127	15 May 52	Column 7 Sec. II Page 5	Column 5 Sec. III Page 10
Service Battery, 112th Field Artillery Battalion	6-129	15 May 52	Column 7 Sec. II	Column 5 Sec. III
130th Antiaircraft Artillery Battalion (Automatic Weapons) (Self-Propelled)	44-75	15 May 52	Column 7 Sec. II Page 6	Column 5 Sec. III Page 13
Hq. Hq. Battery, 130th Antiaircraft Artillery Bn. (Automatic Weapons) (Self-Propelled)	44-76	15 May 52	Column 7 Sec. II	Column 5 Sec. III Page 10
Battery A, 130th Antiaircraft Artillery Bn. (Automatic Weapons) (Self-Propelled)	44-77	15 May 52	Column 7 Sec. II	Column 5 Sec. III
Battery B, 130th Antiaircraft Artillery Bn. (Automatic Weapons) (Self-Propelled)	44-77	15 May 52	Column 7 Sec. II	Column 5 Sec. III
Battery C, 130th Antiaircraft Artillery Bn. (Automatic Weapons) (Self-Propelled)	44-77	15 May 52	Column 7 Sec. II	Column 5 Sec. III
Battery D, 130th Antiaircraft Artillery Bn. (Automatic Weapons) (Self-Propelled)	44-77	15 May 52	Column 7 Sec. II	Column 5 Sec. III

2. The provisions of NGB Circular No. 22, dated 24 September 1948, apply to this reorganization.

3. The number of grades for each MOS, as shown in columns 16 through 21, inclusive (Section II, Organization), are authorized provided the total enlisted

strength does not exceed the total shown in column 8. Personnel rendered surplus by this reorganization will be governed by the provisions of paragraph 6, NGR 15 and paragraph 20, NGR 130.

4. Since the T/O&Es referred to above include a Section III (Equipment) and such Section contains a full strength allowance column (column 4) and a reduced strength allowance column (column 5), National Guard Reduction Tables now being followed (for equipment only) will no longer be required nor be in effect on and after the date of reorganization.

By Order of the Governor:

OFFICIAL
THOMAS B. LONGEST
Military Operations Officer
Adjutant General's Department

JOHN H. MANNING
Major General
The Adjutant General

STATE OF NORTH CAROLINA
ADJUTANT GENERAL'S DEPARTMENT
RALEIGH

GENERAL ORDERS
No. 34

30 December 1952

Reorganization of Communications Augmentation, 156th Fighter Bomber Squadron, NC ANG

1. Pursuant to authority contained in letter, Departments of the Army and the Air Force, National Guard Bureau, file NG-AFOTP, subject: "Reorganization of Communications Augmentation and Communications Squadrons," dated 7 November 1952, the Communications Augmentation of the 156th Fighter Interceptor Squadron is hereby reorganized in accordance with T/O indicated below, effective 1 January 1953.

T/O	Date	Composition	*Authorized*	
			Off	Amn
1-2233	1 Jan. 52	1 x Parts IIC, IIP, IIV, IIY, IIAN, IIAP, IIAU	—	19

Reorganization of Air Police Augmentation, 156th Fighter Bomber Squadron, NC ANG

2. Pursuant to authority contained in letter, Departments of the Army and the Air Force, National Guard Bureau, file NG-AFOTP, subject: "Reorganization of Air Police Augmentation and Air Police Squadrons," dated 7 November 1952, the Air Police Augmentation of the 156th Fighter Interceptor Squadron is hereby reorganized in accordance with T/O indicated below, effective 1 January 1953.

T/O	Date	Composition	Authorized Off	Am
1-8035	1 Apr. 52	1 x Parts IIE, IIG, IIH; 2 x Part IIF	1	26

By Order of the Governor:

OFFICIAL
WILLARD R. BLOXTON
Military Executive Officer
Adjutant General's Department

JOHN H. MANNING
Major General
The Adjutant General

TOTAL NUMBER OF OFFICERS AND ENLISTED MEN WHO ATTENDED SERVICE SCHOOL 1951-1952

Calendar Year 1951

Officers 95
EM 541
          Total 646

Calendar Year 1952

Officers 76
EM 147
          Total 223

1952—CERTAIN IMPORTANT SPECIAL ORDERS AND LETTERS

State of North Carolina
Adjutant General's Department
Raleigh

Special Orders
No. 3

2 January 1952

PAC NGR-20 11 Dec 47 COL CLAUDE T BOWERS 0 183 291 GSC NC NG apt Brig Gen of the line NCNG and asgd C G (SSN 0002) in lieu of Major Gen Hq 30th Inf Div (In Part) NCNG sta Raleigh NC vice Major Gen John H. Manning 0 207 814 reasg *EDCSA 2 Jan 52.*

By Order of the Governor:

OFFICIAL:
David W. Donovan
Military Personnel Officer
The Adjutant General's Department

John H. Manning
Major General
The Adjutant General

State of North Carolina
Adjutant General's Department
Raleigh

EXTRACT

Special Orders
No. 83

7 February 1952

6. PAC NGR-20 11 Dec 47 COL EDWARD F GRIFFIN 0 198 652 Arty NCNG is rel of further asg as (CO) Ex (SSN 1193) Hq 30th Div Arty (In Part) NCNG sta Louisburg NC *eff 6 Feb 52* and asg CO (SSN 0002) in lieu of Brig Gen Hq Hq Btry IV Corps Arty NCNG sta Louisburg NC vice Col Paul R Younts 0 185 367 resigned. Completion and/or distr of DA AGO Form 67-2 and NGB Form-23 UP NGR-21 24 Jul 51 and NGR-23 13 Jun 50 respectively.

7. PAC NGR-20 11 Dec 47 COL EDWARD F GRIFFIN 0 198 652 asg CO (SSN 0002) Hq Hq Btry IV Corps Arty NCNG is apt Brig Gen of the line NCNG *eff 7 Feb 52.*

By Order of the Governor:

OFFICIAL:
David W. Donovan
Military Personnel Officer
The Adjutant General's Department

John H. Manning
Major General
The Adjutant General

REPORT OF THE ADJUTANT GENERAL

STATE OF NORTH CAROLINA
ADJUTANT GENERAL'S DEPARTMENT
RALEIGH

SPECIAL ORDERS   12 March 1952
No.   106

EXTRACT

2. PAC Section VI, NGR 44, dated 6 September 1951, a Board of Officers is appointed to select the most outstanding company-size Army unit of the North Carolina National Guard to be awarded the Eisenhower Trophy for Calendar Year 1951.

DETAIL FOR THE BOARD

Major General John H. Manning, The Adjutant General, North Carolina

Brigadier General Claude T. Bowers, Commanding General, 30th Infantry Division, NCNG

Colonel Lee C. Bizzell, Senior Army Instructor, North Carolina National Guard

By Order of the Governor:

OFFICIAL:
THOMAS B. LONGEST
Military Personnel Officer
The Adjutant General's Department

JOHN H. MANNING
Major General
The Adjutant General

STATE OF NORTH CAROLINA
ADJUTANT GENERAL'S DEPARTMENT
RALEIGH

SPECIAL ORDERS   8 April 1952
No.   124

EXTRACT

6. Under provisions of Par. 1a (2), AR- 20-5, 22 April 1948, and Par. 11, NGR 15, 25 June 1948, an inspection for Federal recoginatiou of Comapny B, 167th MP Battalion, NCNG, station Lasker, North Carolina, will be conducted by an officer designated by the Commanding General, Third Army, Fort McPherson, Georgia.

1st Lt Walter H. Beale, Jr., MPC, NCNG, will present the unit for this inspection according to the following schedule:

    Date: 10 April 1952
    Time: Armory, Records and Personnel—2000 hours
    Place: Armory, Lasker, North Carolina

Necessary records will be prepared and presented to the Inspecting Officer as follows:

a. Copy of letter of authorization to organize the unit and applicable T/O&E from the Office of the Chief, NGB, to The Adjutant General of North Carolina. Five (5) copies.
b. Initial roster of unit WD NGB Form 100. Five (5) copies.
c. Special Orders assigning individual officers to the unit and duties therein. Five (5) copies.
d. Enlistment record WD NGB Form 21 for each member executed in three (3) copies to be completed.
e. Service record NGB Form 24, for each member to be completed to date.

The expense enjoined is necessary in the military service.

By Order of the Governor:

OFFICIAL:
THOMAS B. LONGEST
Military Personnel Officer
The Adjutant General's Department

JOHN H. MANNING
Major General
The Adjutant General

STATE OF NORTH CAROLINA
ADJUTANT GENERAL'S DEPARTMENT
RALEIGH

SPECIAL ORDERS
No.   139

30 April 1952

EXTRACT

24. PAC NGR-20 11 Dec 47 and Ltr NG-AROTO 325.3-Gen Subject: "Allotment of Positions, Headquarters, 30th Inf Div" dtd 21 Apr 52 BRIG GEN CLAUDE T BOWERS 0 183 291 is rel of further asg as CG (SSN 0002) in lieu of Major General Hq 30th Inf Div *eff 30 Apr 52* and asg Asst Div Comd (SSN 0002) Hq 30th Inf Div vice original vacancy upon reorganization.

25. BRIG GEN CLAUDE T BOWERS 0 183 291 Asst Div Comd Hq 30th Inf Div is designated as CG Hq 30th Inf Div (In Part) NCNG in addition to his other duties *eff 1 May 52.*

By Order of the Governor:

OFFICIAL:
DAVID W. DONOVAN
Military Personnel Officer
The Adjutant General's Department

JOHN H. MANNING
Major General
The Adjutant General

STATE OF NORTH CAROLINA
ADJUTANT GENERAL'S DEPARTMENT
RALEIGH

SPECIAL ORDERS
No.   141

2 May 1952

EXTRACT

3. So much of Par 24 SO 139 AGD NC 30 Apr 52 pert to BRIG GEN CLAUDE T BOWERS 0 183 291 as reads "Subject: "Allotment of Positions,

REPORT OF THE ADJUTANT GENERAL 95

Headquarters 30th Inf Div *dtd 12 Apr 52*" is AMENDED to read "Subject: 'Allotment of Positions, Headquarters, 30th Inf Div' *dtd 29 Apr 52*".

By Order of the Governor:

OFFICIAL:
DAVID W. DONOVAN
Military Personnel Officer
The Adjutant General's Department

JOHN H. MANNING
Major General
The Adjutant General

STATE OF NORTH CAROLINA
ADJUTANT GENERAL'S DEPARTMENT
RALEIGH

SPECIAL ORDERS
No. 169

12 June 1952

EXTRACT

1. PAC TA No. 31-B, as amended, National Guard Bureau, dated 7 May 1952, the following Officer, Warrant Officer and EM, NCNG, station and unit indicated, w/p on 2 July 1952 to Fort McClellan, Alabama, reporting upon arrival to the Commanding Officer, Pre-Camp Mess Detachment, to attend the Pre-Camp Mess Training Course for duration of four days, beginning 3 July 1952:

Name	Rank	Sn	Unit	Station	No. Meals
Liles, Graydon C.	1st Lt.	0986482	Hq. 30th Inf. Div. (In Part)	Raleigh, N. C.	0
Cundiff, Louis M., Jr.	WOJG (W-1)	W2006481	Svc. Co., 120th Inf.	Asheville, N. C.	0
Wilson, Joseph N.	M. Sgt	24966755	Co. A, 119th Inf.	Oxford, N. C.	1
Arrington, William G.	SFC	20454455	Tank Co. (Med) 129th Inf.	Waynesville, N. C.	3
Barbee, Calvin J.	SFC	34679356	Co. F, 120th Inf.	Albemarle, N. C.	1
Burns, Claude L.	SFC	20448953	Co. D, 119th Inf.	Durham, N. C.	1
Duncan, Melvin B.	SFC	24966706	Co. A, 119th Inf.	Oxford, N. C.	1
Duggins, Joe E.	SFC	34776599	Co. B, 120th Inf.	Winston-Salem, N. C.	2
Fletcher, James O.	SFC	20453836	Co. E, 120th Inf.	Concord, N. C.	1
Flynt, Harry C.	SFC	24984923	Co. D, 120th Inf.	Winston-Salem, N. C.	2
Gentry, Herbert M.	SFC	24999116	Btry. C, 113th FA Bn.	Roxboro, N. C.	2
Hall, Clyde	SFC	34674882	Co. A, 120th Inf.	Burlington, N. C.	1
Liles, Howard	SFC	25040644	Hq. 30th Inf. Div. (In Part)	Raleigh, N. C.	1
McMillan, David V.	SFC	24965512	Tank Co., (Med) 119th Inf.	Parkton, N. C.	2
Puett, Edward P.	SFC	24995106	Co. L. 120th Inf.	Morganton, N. C.	2
Shumate, Garland C.	SFC	7081235	Hv. Mtr. Co., 120th Inf.	Leaksville, N. C.	2
Womack, Larken B.	SFC	24981510	Svc. Co., 120th Inf.	Asheville, N. C.	3
Agner, Harry L.	Sgt.	24990621	Co. G, 120th Inf.	Salisbury, N. C.	1
Benson, William H.	Sgt.	24980000	Med. Co. 120th Inf.	Mocksville, N. C.	2
Clark, Clarence W.	Sgt.	24988503	Co. E, 120th Inf.	Concord, N. C.	1
Cockrell, William A.	Sgt.	24973346	Co. G, 119th Inf.	Rocky Mt., N. C.	2
Craddock, Henry E.	Sgt.	34996868	Hq. Hq. Co., 1st Bn. 120th Inf.	Mt. Airy, N. C.	2
Davis, William H.	Sgt.	24979919	Co. B, 120th Inf.	Winston-Salem, N. C.	2
Davis, William H.	Sgt.	34895536	Co. K, 120th Inf.	Gastonia, N. C.	1
Dyer, Jack R.	Sgt.	24982207	Hv. Mtr. Co., 120th Inf.	Leaksville, N. C.	2
Eason, Eugene H.	Sgt.	24975937	Co. I, 119th Inf.	Wilmington, N. C.	2
Evans, Ralph H.	Sgt.	34451817	Co. H, 119th Inf.	Scotland Neck, N. C.	2
Goodwin, Willard H.	Sgt.	24964965	Hv. Mtr. Co., 119th Inf.	Edenton, N. C.	2
Hall, Curtis C.	Sgt.	24981807	Svc. Co., 120th Inf.	Asheville, N. C.	3

REPORT OF THE ADJUTANT GENERAL

Name	Rank	SN	Unit	Station	No. Meals
Hawley, Leon L.	Sgt.	24963355	Co. D, 119th Inf.	Durham, N. C.	1
Hefner, Gaither C.	Sgt.	24991597	Co. H, 120th Inf.	Hickory, N. C.	2
Helms, Jesse L.	Sgt.	34772912	Co. K, 120th Inf.	Gastonia, N. C.	1
Hollingsworth, Ernest B.	Sgt.	13277681	Co. B, 167th MP Bn.	Lasker, N. C.	2
Ingle, Calvin C.	Sgt.	14030550	Hq. 30th Sig. Co.	Canton, N. C.	3
Ivey, Wilton G.	Sgt.	24965622	Tank Co., (Med) 119th Inf.	Parkton, N. C.	2
Kearney, William D.	Sgt.	24978052	Co. L, 119th Inf.	Goldsboro, N. C.	2
King, Robert E.	Sgt.	24960655	Hq. Co., 30th Inf. Div.	Apex, N. C.	1
Lowman, Winfred T.	Sgt.	24991646	Co. H, 120th Inf.	Hickory, N. C.	2
Melton, Gaither E.	Sgt.	24999187	Btry. C, 113th FA Bn.	Roxboro, N. C.	2
Orrell, Howard O.	Sgt.	34964569	Co. G. 120th Inf.	Salisbury, N. C.	1
Parker, Cecil L.	Sgt.	20411293	Co. E. 119th Inf.	Roanoke Rapids, N. C.	1
Parker, Joseph T.	Sgt.	24974371	Co. H, 119th Inf.	Scotland Neck, N. C.	2
Rasberry, Donald R.	Sgt.	44079287	Hq. Hq. Co., 1st Bn. 119th Inf.	Durham, N. C.	1
Robinson, Grover K.	Sgt.	20454525	Tank Co. (Med) 120th Inf.	Waynesville, N. C.	3
Roughton, Jack, L.	Sgt.	24971458	Co. E. 119th Inf.	Roanoke Rapids, N. C.	1
Shook, John H.	Sgt.	34894672	Co. I, 120th Inf.	Newton, N. C.	2
Smathers, Sammy J.	Sgt.	44159236	Hq. 30th Signal Co.	Canton, N. C.	3
Vaughn, Bernie W.	Sgt.	24983332	Hq. Hq. Co., 1st Bn. 120th Inf.	Mt. Airy, N.C.	2
Warren, Walter H.	Sgt.	44079753	Med. Co., 120th Inf.	Mocksville, N. C.	2
Whitley, Walter K.	Sgt.	24989547	Co. F, 120th Inf.	Albemarle, N. C.	1
Wood, Edward L.	Sgt.	24998573	Btry. B, 113th FA Bn.	Dunn, N. C.	2
Austin, Billy M.	Cpl.	24993172	Co. I, 120th Inf	Newton, N. C.	2
Bennett, James L.	Cpl.	24997209	Hq. Hq. Btry., 113th FA Bn.	Louisburg, N. C.	1
Bright, Erna D.	Cpl.	24964360	Svc. Co., 119th Inf.	Eilzabeth City, N. C.	2
Clark, Bobby B.	Cpl.	25150708	Co. F, 119th Inf.	Tarboro, N. C.	2
Crowder, Philip L.	Cpl.	24973420	Co. G, 119th Inf.	Rocky Mt, N. C.	2
Davis, Authur D.	Cpl.	24987915	Hq. Hq. Co., 2nd Bn. 120th Inf.	Asheboro, N. C.	1
Frank, Hobert L.	Cpl.	24986059	Co. C, 120th Inf.	Lexington, N. C.	1
Hall, Grover M.	Cpl.	24979054	Co. M. 119th Inf.	Warsaw, N. C.	3
Howard, Lellyn	Cpl.	44087830	Co. L, 120th Inf.	Morganton, N. C.	2
Howington, Charles W.	Cpl.	24960652	Hq. Co., 30th Inf. Div.	Apex, N. C.	1
Jernigan, Wade L.	Cpl.	25037005	Co. A, 167th MP Bn.	Windsor, N. C.	1
Johnson, Tremain R.	Cpl.	24972367	Co. F, 119th Inf.	Tarboro, N. C.	2
Jones, Ernest	Cpl.	6887473	Co. I, 119th Inf.	Wilmington, N. C.	2
Lane, Archie. T., Jr.	Cpl.	24964975	Hv. Mtr. Co., 119th Inf.	Edenton, N. C.	2
Mercer, Charles D.	Cpl.	24962791	Med. Co., 119th Inf.	Wilson, N. C.	2
Moore, Willie C.	Cpl.	24998651	Btry. B, 113th FA Bn.	Dunn, N. C.	1
Murphy, Bruce E.	Cpl.	24968854	Co. B, 119th Inf.	Warrenton, N. C.	1
Peele, Leon M.	Cpl.	25036608	Hq. Hq. Co., 167th MP Bn.	Ahoskie, N. C.	2
Pope, Robert D.	Cpl.	24975427	Hq. Hq. Co., 3rd Bn. 119th Inf.	Clinton, N. C.	3
Poulos, Richard E.	Cpl.	24964430	Svc. Co., 119th Inf.	Elizabeth City, N. C.	2
Register, Corbet H.	Cpl.	24979122	Co. M, 119th Inf.	Warsaw, N. C.	3
Robinson, Joseph	Cpl.	24967821	Co. B, 119th Inf.	Warrenton, N. C.	1
Soyars, David M.	Cpl.	24980690	Hq. Hq. Co., 120th Inf.	Reidsville, N. C.	1
Spivey, Jimmy W.	Cpl.	24997903	Btry. A, 113th FA Bn.	Zebulon, N. C.	1
Teague, Bill B.	Cpl.	24987906	Hq. Hq. Co., 2nd Bn. 120th Inf.	Asheboro, N. C.	1
Thrift, Allen I	Cpl.	20454933	Co. M, 120th Inf.	Shelby, N. C.	1
Valentine, Ernest P.	Cpl.	24997234	Hq. Hq. Btry., 113th FA Bn.	Louisburg, N. C.	1
Weathers, Willis P.	Cpl.	24999728	Svc. Btry. 113th FA Bn.	Youngsville, N. C.	1
White, Verlon D.	Cpl.	25037007	Co. A, 167th MP Bn.	Windsor, N. C.	2
Askew, Leonard H.	Pfc	24999761	Svc. Btry, 113th FA Bn.	Youngsville, N. C.	1
Beddingfield, Clarence L.	Pfc	24997944	Btry. A, 113th FA Bn.	Zebulon, N. C.	1
Edmonds, Lewis H.	Pfc	24984118	Co. A, 120th Inf.	Burlington, N. C.	1
Fisher, Lewis E.	Pfc	24996327	Co. M, 120th Inf.	Shelby, N. C.	1
Oakley, Franklin, G.	Pfc	24963445	Hq. Hq. Co., 119th Inf.	Durham, N. C.	1
Powell, James T.	Pfc	24977007	Co. K, 119th Inf.	Fayetteville, N. C.	2
Pryor, Dewey L.	Pfc	24980689	Hq. Hq. Co., 120th Inf.	Reidsville, N. C.	1
Rathbone, Stephen E.	Pfc	24992538	Hq. Hq. Co., 3rd Bn. 120th Inf.	Kings Mtn, N. C.	1.
Weinberg, Robert L.	Pfc	24977022	Co. K, 119th Inf.	Fayetteville, N. C.	2
Barefoot, John T.	Pvt. (E-2)	24975448	Hq. Hq. Co., 3rd Bn., 119th Inf.	Clinton, N. C.	3

Report of the Adjutant General 97

Name	Rank	SN	Uni	Station	No. Meals
Ellis, Mickey W.	Pvt. (E-2)	24963452	Hq. Hq. Co., 119th Inf.	Durham, N. C.	1
Gurley, Woodard H.	Pvt. (E-2)	24978157	Co. L, 119th Inf.	Goldsboro, N. C.	2
Harper, Richard W. H., Jr.	Pvt. (E-2)	24966188	Hq. Hq. Co., 1st Bn., 119th Inf.	Durham, N. C.	1
Johnson, Cecil C.	Pvt. (E-2)	25036610	Hq. Hq. Co., 167th MP Bn.	Ahoskie, N. C.	2
Ramsey, Fred W.	Pvt. (E-2)	24922578	Hq. Hq. Co,. 3rd Bn., 120th Inf.	Kings Mtn, N. C.	1
Steelman, William H.	Pvt. (E-2)	24987001	Co. D, 120th Inf.	Winston-Salem, N. C.	2
Lamn, Marshall L.	Pvt. (E-1)	24962822	Med. Co., 119th Inf.	Wilson, N. C.	2
Wheeler, Eston L.	Pvt. (E-1)	25036618	Co. B, 167th MP Bn.	Lasker, N. C.	2

2. Upon the completion of the above training o/a 6 July 1952, personnel will report to their respective unit commanders at Fort McClellan, Alabama to participate in Field Training for a period of 15 days.

3. TR to be issued by Acting USP & DO, North Carolina. It being impracticable to furnish subsistence in kind while traveling, each EM listed above is authorized monetary allowances in lieu of subsistence for the number of meals listed at .86¢ per meal or $2.57 per day.

4. TDN 212/32060 18-1131 P1110-01 S31-079
212/32060 18-1431 P1140-08 S31-079
212/32060 18-1631 P1160-02 S31-079
2122020 18-6731 P1670-07 S31-079

By Order of the Governor:

OFFICIAL:
WILLARD R. BLOXTON
Military Operations Officer
The Adjutant General's Department

JOHN H. MANNING
Major General
The Adjutant General

STATE OF NORTH CAROLINA
ADJUTANT GENERAL'S DEPARTMENT
RALEIGH

SPECIAL ORDERS   25 June 1952
No.   179

EXTRACT

1. So much of S. O. No. 169, this Department, dated 12 June 1952, pertaining to Pre-Camp Mess Training Course, Fort McClellan, Alabama for certain personnel, NCNG, as reads, "18-1131, 18-1431, 18-1631, 2122020" is AMENDED to read, "18-1731, 18-1831, 18-1931, 2132020".

By Order of the Governor:

OFFICIAL:
WILLARD R. BLOXTON
Military Executive Officer
The Adjutant General's Department

JOHN H. MANNING
Major General
The Adjutant General

REPORT OF THE ADJUTANT GENERAL

STATE OF NORTH CAROLINA
ADJUTANT GENERAL'S DEPARTMENT
RALEIGH

SPECIAL ORDERS 23 June 1952
No. 177

EXTRACT

1. PAC TA No. 31-A, as amended, National Guard Bureau, dated 25 April 1952, the following officers and EM, NCNG, station and unit indicated, w/p on 9 July 1952 to Fort McClellan, Alabama, reporting upon arrival to the Commanding Officer, Pre-Camp Mess Detachment, to attend the Pre-Camp Mess Training Course for duration of four days, beginning 10 July 1952:

Name	Rank	SN	Unit	Station	No. Meals
Shaw, Victor Jr.	Capt.	0-541382	Hq. Hq. Btry. IV Corps Arty.	Charlotte, N. C.	0
Morse, Harris A.	2nd Lt.	0-2263927	Hq. Hq. Btry. IV Corps Arty.	Charlotte, N. C.	0
Preswell, Henry W.	SFC	14037614	Btry. C, 505th FA Bn.	Greensboro, N. C.	1
Stillwell, James E.	SFC	34592160	Hq. Hq. Btry. IV Corps Arty.	Charlotte, N. C.	1
Britt, Luby R.	Sgt.	25034904	Btry. A, 505th FA Bn.	Greensboro, N. C.	1
Eldins, Ralph W.	Sgt.	25023567	3624th Ord. Med. Maint. Co.	Butner, N. C.	
Osborne, Ansel L.	Sgt.	25033826	Hq. Hq. Btry., 505th FA Bn.	Greensboro, N. C.	1
Smith, Beauford R.	Sgt.	25036116	Svc. Btry., 505th FA Bn.	Greensboro, N. C.	1
Troxler, James N.	Sgt.	25034302	Hq. Hq. Btry., 252nd FA Gp.	Greensboro, N. C.	1
Wagner, Elijah L.	Sgt.	34851494	3624th Ord. Med. Maint. Co.	Butner, N. C.	
Boone, Carl V.	Cpl.	53024047	Btry. B, 505th FA Bn.	Greensboro, N. C.	1
Causey, Charles W.	Cpl.	25036121	Svc. Btry., 505th FA Bn.	Greensboro, N. C.	1
Elam, Louis B.	Cpl.	25024350	Hq. Hq. Btry, IV Corps Arty.	Charlotte, N. C.	1
Thompson, Robert B.	Cpl.	25034351	Btry. A. 505th FA Bn.	Greensboro, N. C.	1
Barbour, Charles D.	Pfc	25034975	Btry. B, 505th FA Bn.	Greensboro, N. C.	1
Peoples, Clayton D.	Pfc	25035515	Btry. C, 505th FA Bn.	Greensboro, N. C.	1
Meadows, Herbert L.	Pfc	25033722	Hq. Hq. Btry., 252nd FA Gp.	Greensboro, N. C.	1
Sugg, Henry C.	Pfc.	25025591	Hq. Hq. Btry., 196th FA Gp.	Kinston, N. C.	2
Wosham, William E.	Pvt-2	25033885	Hq. Hq. Btry., 505th FA Bn.	Greensboro, N. C.	1
Richardson, Robert T.	Pvt-1	25024386	Hq. Hq. Btry., IV Corps Arty.	Charlotte, N. C.	1

Upon completion of above training o/a 13 July 1952, personnel will report to their respective unit commanders at Fort McCellan, Alabama to participate in Field Training for a period of 15 days. TR to be issued by Acting USP & Do, North Carolina. It being impracticable to furnish subsistence in kind while traveling each EM listed above is authorized monetary allowances in lieu of subsistence for the number of meals listed at .86¢ per meal or $2.57 per day.

```
TDN   212/32060   18-1731   P1110-01   S31-079
      212/32060   18-1831   P1140-08   S31-079
      212/32060   18-1931   P1160-02   S31-079
      2132020    18-6731   P1670-07   S31-079
```

By Order of the Governor:

JOHN H. MANNING
Major General
The Adjutant General

OFFICIAL:
WILLARD R. BLOXTON
Military Executive Officer
The Adjutant General's Department

REPORT OF THE ADJUTANT GENERAL

STATE OF NORTH CAROLINA
ADJUTANT GENERAL'S DEPARTMENT
RALEIGH

SPECIAL ORDERS   1 July 1952
No.   183

26. So much of Par 1, SO 177, this Dept, dtd 23 Jun 52, as reads, "Barbour, Charles D Pfc 25034975 Btry B 505th FA Bn Greensboro NC 1" is AMENDED to read, "Thacker, Claude D Pfc 25034916 Btry B 505th FA Bn Greensboro NC 1."

By Order of the Governor:

JOHN H. MANNING
Major General
The Adjutant General

OFFICIAL

WILLARD R. BLOXTON
Military Executive Officer
Adjutant General's Department

STATE OF NORTH CAROLINA
ADJUTANT GENERAL'S DEPARTMENT
RALEIGH

SPECIAL ORDERS   26 June 1952
No.   180

EXTRACT

16. With profound sorrow the death of 1ST LT HILDRETH LACUE PAYNE JR AO 941 599 Pilot 156th Ftr Sq NCANG on 7 Jun 1952 is announced.

Lt Payne was born in Boston, Massachusetts on 21 November 1924, lived in Hyde Park Mass until 1949 when he moved to Charlotte NC where he joined the Associated Press Bureau. Lt Payne was a graduate of Hyde Park High School and Boston University receiving a BS in Journalism in 1949.

Lt Payne was a young man of sterling qualities, he was admired by and had the confidence of those with whom he came in contact. In his sudden death his community lost a valued citizen. The Armed Forces has lost a most valuable efficient and faithful officer.

Record of Military Service.—Lt Payne served in the Air Corps Enlisted Reserve during the period of 14 December 1942 through 22 February 1943. On 23 February 1943 he entered into active Federal service as an Air-Cadet receiving the grade of Flight Officer 5 August 1944. Upon release from active Federal service 18 September 1946 he was transferred to the AAF Reserve Corps receiving an appointment as 2nd Lt on 20 December 1946. On 3 January 1947 Lt Payne was appointed as 2nd Lt in the Massachusetts National Guard serving with the 67th Ftr Wing and 101st Ftr Squadron until 1 June 1949 at which time his appointment was terminated because of change of residence to Charlotte NC. On 2 June 1949 Lt Payne was appointed as 2nd Lt North Carolina National Guard and assigned as Pilot (SSN 1054) 156th Ftr Squadron NC ANG station Charlotte NC. Lt Payne was promoted to 1st Lt NC ANG on 13 September 1950 and entered active Federal service in that grade on 10 October 1950 as a member of 156th Ftr Squadron NC ANG. Lt Payne was killed while piloting a F-51 Mustang over Tokyo on 7 June 1952.

Next of kin.—Mrs. Mollie N. Payne wife 18 Morse Avenue Dedham Massachusetts.

By Order of the Governor:

OFFICIAL
DAVID W. DONOVAN
Military Executive Officer
Adjutant General's Department

JOHN H. MANNING
Major General
The Adjutant General

REPORT OF THE ADJUTANT GENERAL

DETACHMENT 9 ASU 3320
National Guard Instructor Group
North Carolina Military District
Post Office Box 791
Raleigh, North Carolina

GENERAL ORDERS
NUMBER   1

1 July 1952

ASSUMPTION OF COMMAND

Under the provisions of paragraph 4, AR 600-20, the undersigned hereby assumes command of Detachment 9, ASU 3320, National Guard Instructor Group, North Carolina Military District.

WILLIAM R. WATSON
Colonel, Infantry
Commanding

DISTRIBUTION:
  A B M
INFORMATION:
  C F
  Mil Dist (10)

---

13 March 1952   JHM/dcw

SUBJECT: Commendation for Colonel Lee C. Bizzell, Senior Instructor, North Carolina National Guard.

TO: The Adjutant General
Department of the Army
The Pentagon
Washington 25, D. C.

THRU: The Chief, National Guard Bureau
Depts of the Army and the Air Force
The Pentagon
Washington 25, D. C.

1. As the normal tour of duty of Colonel Lee C. Bizzell, 0-10250, Infantry, Senior Instructor, North Carolina National Guard, draws to a close, I wish to record my appreciation of the very fine services rendered to the North Carolina National Guard by Colonel Bizzell during the past nearly three years. He has been earnest, conscientious, and hard working with his sole interest being the promotion and betterment of the North Carolina National Guard. His services in this particular have been outstanding. He has been most helpful and cooperative in every way and has done his work in a most gracious manner.

2. It is with much regret that the normal tour of duty of Colonel Bizzell will be reached in August, and that he will leave North Carolina for another assignment.

JOHN H. MANNING
Major General
The Adjutant General

REPORT OF THE ADJUTANT GENERAL

FINANCE OFFICE
HEADQUARTERS, THIRD ARMY

FINKE—AA 240.9(NG) 29 August 1952

National Guard Payments
The Adjutant General
State of North Carolina
P O Box 791
Raleigh, North Carolina

1. Reference your telegram received 27 August 1952 regarding amount of money received by personnel of North Carolina National Guard for participating in Armory Drill during Fiscal Years 1948 through 1952.

2. Figures for the period prior to 1 July 1949 are not available. Listed below are approximate figures, separated to show amounts for Armory Drill and Field Training according to Fiscal Years. Included in Armory Drill figure is Week-End Range Firing and Inactive Duty Training (OUTDOOR). Included in Field Training are Staff Schools and other types of duty reported on Field Training forms.

1 July 49—30 Jun 50		1 Jul 50—30 Jun 51		1 Jul 51—30 Jun 52	
AD	FT	AD	FT	AD	FT
$992,971.73	12,804.36	1,286,450.77	409,617.49	1,225,380.74	420,436.00

J. B. REGAN
Lt Col, FC
Finance Officer.

STATE OF NORTH CAROLINA
ADJUTANT GENERAL'S DEPARTMENT
RALEIGH

27 June 1952

SUBJECT: Compensation for FY 1953 of Employees Paid with Federal Funds

TO: All Federally Paid Employees
All Unit Commanders

1. The allotment of funds by the National Guard Bureau for the fiscal year ending 30 June 1953 is insufficient to meet payroll requirements for the following personnel:

42	Employees	Office of USP & DO, SMO, USP & DO Warehouse
3	"	SMP (NGC Clerks)
37	"	State Maint. Pool Mechanics (NGM)
13½	"	Army Aviation
94	"	Adm. Assts. (Officers & NCOs)
80	"	Mechanics, General (Caretakers)
8	"	Service Center Mechanics
1	"	Range Keeper

278½ Total Employees

2. The Chief, National Guard Bureau informed the Adjutant General that additional funds were not in prospect and the adjustments necessary to keep payroll requirements within allotted funds should be made effective 1 July 1952, the beginning of the fiscal year. Any solution to bring payroll requirements within allotted funds was so important that the Adjutant General called a meeting of the Advisory Council, which was held on 16 June 1952 and attended by eleven (11) senior officers representing all units of the North Carolina National Guard. The AAA units were in field training at Camp Stewart, Ga., and were not represented.

3. After more than three hours of discussion, the following recommendations were adopted unanimously by the Advisory Council:

(1) That the following positions now authorized not be filled:
One Clerk, Supply, Grade NGC 7, Office of the USP & DO
One Clerk, NGC 5, SMP
One Mechanic, NGM 15, SMP
One One-half (½) time A & E Mechanic, Army Aviation
One Caretaker
One Service Center Mechanic, NGM 15

(2) That merit increases for State Maintenance Pool and Army Aviation personnel be granted during FY 1953 when eligible.

(3) That raises be allowed twenty-seven (27) unit caretakers now paid below the present maximum.

(4) That minor adjustments be made for one employee, Office USP & DO, two (2) employees, Warehouse USP & DO and that no across the board cut be made in the compensation now paid to five (5) Truck Drivers—material handlers—USP & DO Warehouse now being paid below maximum.

(5) That no other increases, merit or step, be granted during FY 1953.

(6) That the deficit resulting from application of (1), (2), (3), (4) and (5) be eliminated by a straight five (5) per cent across the board salary reduction on all employees, effective 1 July 1952.

(7) That further adjustments, if necessary, be made in the third and fourth quarters or in the fourth quarter in the discretion of the Adjutant General and the USP & DO.

(8) That in the event additional funds become available, the salary cuts be restored and increases granted where merited or entitled to the extent possible.

4. The Adjutant General approved the recommendations of the Advisory Council. The Adjutant General wishes to record his appreciation of the very fine service rendered by personnel affected by this salary reduction and to express his regret that such action is necessary. Responsible officers will notify all personnel affected, without delay, of the action set forth in this letter.

JOHN H. MANNING
Major General
The Adjutant General

JHM/mh

Report of the Adjutant General

Report of Active Duty Accomplishments

1. Unit Designation 156th Fighter Squadron Location Morris Fld, Charlotte, N. C.

2. Number of ANG personnel entering Federal service with unit 105

3. Number of ANG personnel return from Federal service 68

4. Zone of Interior:
   Major Command to which Unit was assigned Tactical Air Command
   Location of assignment Godman Air Force Base, Ft. Knox, Ky.
   Primary mission of unit Fighter Bomber

5. Overseas Duty:
   Major Command to which Unit was assigned United States Air Force in Europe
   Theatre or Country England; Primary Mission Fighter Bomber
   Inclusive dates of unit's overseas assignment 7 Nov 51 to 9 Jul 52
   (Unit was redesignated on 10 July 52 as 512th Ftr Bmr Sq)

6. Individual Personnel:
   ANG personnel transferred to other units 79*
   ANG personnel assigned to overseas duty with other units 19
   *Incuudes personnel who did not accompany unit overseas

7. Combat Operations of unit and/or individual ANG personnel:
   Total combat sorties by members of unit 1,048
   Enemy aircraft destroyed None; Damaged None
   Bombs dropped 693 (Approx); Rockets fired 1726 (Approx)
   Napalm dropped 28,600 gals (Approx); cal rounds expended 1,255,750 (Approx)

8. Losses: (Enter number)
   Personnel reported killed in action None
   Personnel reported missing in action None
   Personnel wounded in action None
   Other casualties One Officer killed in aircraft accident in Japan

9. Awards, Decorations, Citation: (Enter *total of all awards* to individuals and to the unit. Include Medal of Honor, DSM, DSC, Legion of Merit, Silver Star, Soldiers Medal, DFC, Purple Heart, Air Medal, Bronze Star, Commendation Ribbon, etc.)
   Awards to individuals 40; Unit Citations None to 156th (12 Officers served with units that were cited in Korea)

10. Outstanding Accomplishments of unit or individuals: —
    Number and Identity of Aces None
    Other outstanding accomplishments —

WILLIAM J. PAYNE, *Lt Col NC ANG*
Commanding, Hq N. C. Air Nat'l Guard

Report of The Adjutant General

Report of Active Duty Accomplishments

1. Unit Designation Utility Flight, 156th Ftr Sq; Location Morris Fld, Charlotte, N. C.

2. Number of ANG personnel entering Federal service with unit 30

3. Number of ANG personnel returned from Federal service 28

4. Zone of Interior:
    Major Commany to which Unit was assigned Tactical Air Command
    Location of assignment Godman AFB, Ft. Knox, Ky.
    Primary mission of unit: This unit was disbanded immediately after recall and members were reassigned to other units in the 123rd Fighter Bomber Wing.

5. Overseas Duty:
    Major Command to which Unit was assigned N/A
    Theatre or Country N/A; Primary Mission N/A
    Inclusive dates of unit's overseas assignment/ NA

6. Individual Personnel:
    ANG personnel transferred to other units 30—see par 4 above
    ANG personnel assigned to overseas duty with other units 2

7. Combat Operations of unit and/or individual ANG personnel:
    Total combat sorties by members of unit 100
    Eenemy aircraft destroyed None; Damaged None
    Bombs dropped 200; Rockets fired 40
    Napalm dropped 1,320 gal; 50 cal rounds expended 100,000

8. Losses: (Enter number)
    Personnel reported killed in action None
    Personnel reported missing in action None
    Personnel wounded in action One
    Other casualties None

9. Awards, Decorations, Citations: (Enter *total of all awards* to individuals and to the unit. Include Medal of Honor, DSM, DSC, Legion of Merit, Silver Star, Soldiers Medal, DFC, Purple Heart, Air Medal, Bronze Star, Commendation Ribbon, etc.)
    Awards to individuals 5; Unit Citations N/A

10. Outstanding Accomplishments of unit or individuals: None
    Number and Identity of Aces None
    Other outstanding accomplishments —

WILLIAM J. PAYNE, *Lt Col NC ANG*
Commanding Hq N. C. Air Nat'l Guard

Report of The Adjutant General

Report of Active Duty Accomplishments

1. Unit Designation 156th Weather Station; Location Morris Field, Charlotte, N. C.

2. Number of ANG personnel entering Federal service with unit 6

3. Number of ANG personnel returned from Federal service 6

4. Zone of Interior:
    Major Command to which Unit was assigned Tactical Air Command
    Location of assignment Godman Air Force Base, Ft. Knox, Ky.
    Primary mission of unit This unit was disbanded immediately after recall and four of the members were accepted by Air Weather Service—Others were reassigned to units of 123rd Ftr Bmr Wg

5. Overseas Duty:
    Major Command to which Unit was assigned N/A
    Theatre or Country N/A; Primary Mission N/A
    Inclusive dates of unit's overseas assignment N/A

6. Individual Personnel:
    ANG personnel transferred to other units 6—see par 4 above
    ANG personnel assigned to overseas duty with other units 0

7. Combat Operations of unit and/or individual ANG personnel:
    Total combat sorties by members of unit None
    Enemy aircraft destroyed None; Damaged None
    Bombs dropped None; Rockets Fired None
    Napalm dropped None; 50 cal rounds expended None

8. Losses: (Enter number)
    Personnel reported killed in action None
    Personnel reported missing in action None
    Personnel wounded in action None
    Other casualties None

9. Awards, Decorations, Citations: (Enter *total of all awards* to individuals and to the unit. Include Medal of Honor, DSM, DSC, Legion of Merit, Silver Star, Soldiers Medal, DFC, Purple Heart, Air Medal, Bronze Star, Commendation Ribbon, etc.)
    Awards to individuals None; Unit Citations None

10. Outstanding Accomplishments of unit or individuals: None
    Number and Identity of Aces None
    Other outstanding accomplishments —

WILLIAM J. PAYNE, *Lt Col NC ANG*
Commanding Hq N. C. Air Nat'l Guard

Report of The Adjutant General

Report of Active Duty Accomplishments

1. Unit Designation Det "C" 218th Air Sv Group; Location Morris Field, Charlotte, N. C.

2. Number of ANG personnel entering Federal service with unit 143

3. Number of Ang personnel returned from Federal service 100

4. Zone of Interior:
    Major Command to which Unit was assigned Tactical Air Command
    Location of assignment Godman Air Force Base, Ft. Knox, Ky.
    Primary mission of unit Disbanded immediately after recall and members were reassigned to support type units in the 123rd Ftr Bmr Wing

5. Overseas Duty:
    Major Command to which Unit was assigned N/A
    Theatre or country N/A; Primary Mission N/A
    Inclusive dates of unit's overseas assignment N/A

6. Individual Personnel:
    ANG personnel transferred to other units 143—see par 4 above
    ANG personnel assigned to overseas duty with other units 10 (Exact number of personnel which accompanied 123rd Ftr Bmr Wing to Europe is unknown)

7. Combat operations of unit and/or individual ANG personnel:
    Total combat sorties by members of unit None
    Enemy aircraft destroyed None; Damaged None
    Bombs dropped None; Rockets fired None
    Napalm dropped None; 50 cal rounds expended None

8. Losses: (Enter number)
    Personnel reported killed in action None
    Personnel reported missing in action None
    Personnel wounded in action None
    Other casualties None

9. Awards, Decorations, Citations: (Enter *total of all awards* to individuals and to the unit. Inctlude Medal of Honor, DSM, DSC, Legion of Merit, Silver Star, Soldiers Medal, DFC, Purple Heart, Air Medal, Bronze Star, Commendation Ribbon, etc.)
    Awards to individuals One; Unit Citations None

10. Outstanding Accomplishments of unit or individuals: None
    Number and Identity of Aces None
    Other outstanding accomplishments —

WILLIAM J. PAYNE, *Lt Col NC ANG*
Commanding Hq N. C. Air Nat'l Guard

Report of The Adjutant General

Report of Active Duty Accomplishments

1. Unit Designation 118th AC & W Squadron; Location Morris Fld, Charlotte, N. C.

2. Number of ANG personnel entering Federal service with unit 167

3. Number of ANG personnel returned from Federal service 148

4. Zone of Interior:
   Major Command to which Unit was assigned Tactical Air Command
   Location of assignment Stewart AFB, Smyrna, Tennessee
   Primary mission of unit Air Defense

5. Overseas Duty:
   Major Command to which unit was assigned USAFE
   Theatre or Country North Africa; Primary Mission Air Defense
   Inclusive dates of Unit's assignment 24 Dec 51 to 7 Oct 52 (Numbered ANG Unit returned to State Control 7 Oct 52, the redesignated unit currently in N. Africa)

6. Individual Personnel:
   ANG personnel transferred to other units 40
   ANG personnel assigned to overseas duty with other units 10

7. Combat Operations of unit and/or individual ANG personnel:
   Total combat sorties by members of unit None
   Enemy aircraft destroyed None; Damaged None
   Bombs dropped None; Rockets fired None
   Napalm dropped None; 50 cal rounds expended None

8. Losses: (Enter number)
   Personnel reported killed in action None
   Personnel reported missing in action None
   Personnel wounded in action None
   Other casualties None

9. Awards, Decorations, Citations: (Enter *total of all awards* to individuals and to the unit. Include Medals of Honor, DSM, DSC, Legion of Merit, Silver Star, Soldiers Medal, DFC, Purple Heart, Air Medal, Bronze Star, Commendation Ribbon, etc.)
   Awards to individuals None; Unit Citations None

10. Outstanding Accomplishments of unit or individuals:
    Number and Identity of Aces None
    Other outstanding accomplishments None

WILLIAM J. PAYNE, *Lt Col NC ANG*
Commanding Hq N. C. Air Nat'l Guard

ROSTER OF OFFICERS AND WARRANT OFFICERS IN THE NORTH CAROLINA NATIONAL GUARD AS OF 31 DECEMBER 1951

ARMY UNITS

(NON-DIV)

Hq Hq Det, NC NG, Raleigh, N. C. (Federally Recognized 18 March 1947)

    Austell, Michael H., Colonel
    Jonas, Charles R., Colonel
    Upton, Thomas H., Colonel
    Broaddus, Russell G., Lt. Colonel
    Bruton, Thomas W., Lt. Colonel
    Cavaness, Hugh L., Lt. Colonel
    Edwards, Daniel K., Lt. Colonel
    Foreman, John, Lt. Colonel
    Hutchinson, Henry H., Lt. Colonel
    Pickens, Wiley M., Lt. Colonel
    Armstrong, Lee Roy W., Major
    Donovan, David W., Major
    Ludwig, Edward W., Major
    Mathis, Quince E., Major
    Ratchford, Charles B., Major
    Reitzel, John L., Major
    Brown, Thomas C., Captain
    Leinster, Joseph A., Captain
    Lewis, Walter C., Captain
    Pait, Neil J. Jr., Captain
    Wilkins, Robert J., Captain
    York, Richard G., Captain
    Carter, Thomas E., 1st Lt.
    Hayes, Grayson, 1st Lt.
    Massengill, Hugh P., 1st Lt.
    Sechriest, Stuart W., 1st Lt.
    Patrick, William L., WOJG (W-1)

(DIV-UNITS)

Hq 30th Inf Div (In Part), NCNG, Raleigh, N. C. (Federally recognized 11 Sept 1947)

    Bowers, Claude T., Colonel
    Davis, Fitzgerald E., Lt. Colonel
    Hatcher, Howell J., Lt. Colonel
    Lee, Joel T., Lt. Colonel
    Longest, Thomas B., Lt. Colonel
    Manning, Howard E., Lt. Colonel
    Shimer, Clarence B., Lt. Colonel
    Currin, Robert G., Major

Davis, Ferd L., Major
Dorsett, James K. Jr., Major
Manooch, Charles S. Jr., Major
Patterson, Eugene R., Major
Smith, Kenneth A., Major
Stott, Charles C., Major
Vinson, James A., Major
Alford, Lonnie R., Captain
Blalock, Clifton E. Jr., Captain
Coxe, James S. Jr., Captain
Harrell, Jesse L., Captain
Holoman, William K., Captain
Shelden, Robert E. H., Captain
Clark, Luther W., 1st Lt.
Marks, Charles L., 1st Lt.
Robinson, Bernard E., 1st Lt.
Gminder, Russell, 2nd Lt.
Liles, Graydon C., 2nd Lt.
Edwards, Robert H. Jr., WOJG (W-1)
Hutton, James L., Jr., WOJG (W-1)
Jones, Donald B., WOJG (W-1)
Pate, Chester E., WOJG (W-1)

Hq Co., NCNG, Apex, N. C. (Federally Recognized 22 March 1948)

Ashley, Jay L., Captain
Bass, Mack G. Jr., Captain
Daughtry, John P. Jr., 1st Lt.
Hutchins, James T., 1st Lt.
King, Edward A., 1st Lt.
Edwards, Everette M., Jr., 2nd Lt.
Elliott, Leighton M., 2nd Lt.
King, Centennial C., 2nd Lt.
Hoffman, Roger B., WOJG (W-1)
Riley, Fred T., WOJG (W-1)

Signal Co., NCNG, Canton, N. . (Federally Recognized 14 May 1947)

Stephenson, Victor S. Jr., Major
Chapman, Weaver C., Captain
Cooper, Woodrow W., Captain
Keylon, Arthur F., 1st Lt.
McKinnish, Roy M., 1st Lt.
Peek, Will W. Jr., 1st Lt.
Smathers, Sigmon W., 1st Lt.
White, James A., 1st Lt.
Russell, Jack H., 2nd Lt.
Snook, Samuel A., Jr., 2nd Lt.
Davis, Stuart M., WOJG (W-1)
Elliz, Horace, WOJG (W-1)

Hq 30th Div Arty (In Part) NCNG, Louisburg, N. C. (Federally Recognized 25 August 1947)

 Griffin, Edward F., Colonel
 Rodman, William B., Captain

Med. Det., Div Hq., NCNG, Apex, N. C. (Federally Recognized 13 January 1950)

 Hart, Lillard F., Captain

119th Infantry

Hq Hq Co, NCNG, Durham, N. C. (Federally Recognized 8 July 1947)

 Hardesty, Ivan, Colonel
 Harrison, George W., Major
 Sanders, Richard T., Major
 Taylor, Herbert H., Jr., Major
 Cartwright, John W., Captain
 Lougee, Henry S., Captain
 Newbold, Jerry M., Chaplain) Captain
 Pickett, Stewart M., Captain
 White-Hurst, Bernard M., (Chaplain) Captain
 Edwards, Arthur T., 1st Lt.
 Cleveland, Robert D., 2nd Lt.
 Hale, Claude E., Jr., 2nd Lt.
 Raynor, George E. Jr., 2nd Lt.
 Scott, Jesse P., 2nd Lt.
 Kaufman, Siegmund, WOJG (W-1)
 Rees, Leland M., WOJG (W-1)

Service Co, NCNG, Elizabeth City, N. C. (Federally Recognizde 8 April 1947)

 Ingram, William E., Major
 Pennington, Hubert E., Captain
 Scott, Shelton G., Captain
 White, Beverly W., Captain
 Chapin, William McC., CWO (W-2)
 Helmkamp, Richard C., WOJG (W-1)
 Perry, William W., WOJG (W-1)

Hv. Mortar Co, NCNG, Edenton, N. C. (Federally Recognized 12 May 1947).

 Fry, Cecil W., 1st Lt.
 Swanner, Charlie W., 1st Lt.
 Moore, Wayland C. Jr., 2nd Lt.
 Asbell, John H. Jr., WOJG (W-1)

Med Tank Co, NCNG, Parkton, N. C. (Federally Recognized 16 September 1947)

  Hall, Roger F., Captain
  Smathers, Rufus E., 1st Lt.
  Wall, Mal L., 1st Lt.
  Acree, Carl L., 2nd Lt.
  McGougan, Ernest D., 2nd Lt.
  Hall, James E. Jr., WOJG (W-1)

Medical Co, NCNG, Wilson, N. C. (Federally Recognized 10 March 1949)

  Hood, John M., Captain
  Taylor, Allen, Captain
  Boyette, Earl R., 2nd Lt.
  Grady, Paul D., 2nd Lt.
  Lamm, John G., 2nd Lt.
  Vick, George C. Jr., 2nd Lt.

Hq Hq Co, 1st Bn, NCNG, Durham, N. C. (Federally Recognized 3 October 1947)

  Steagall, Gordon I., Lt. Colonel
  Floyd, John E., Major
  Sanders, Harper K. Jr., Major
  Barnes, Lee R., Captain
  Bouchard, Arthur J., Captain
  Perry, William E., Jr., Captain
  Chandler, Malcolm T., 2nd Lt.
  Dennis, Luther A., 2nd Lt.
  Dudley, Roland E., 2nd Lt.
  Pickett, Claudius A., 2nd Lt.

Co. A, NCNG, Oxford, N. C. (Federally Recognized 12 May 1947)

  Keeton, William P. Jr., Captain
  East, Thomas F., 1st Lt.
  Hancock, Franklin W. III, 1st Lt.
  Puckett, Hoyle B., 1st Lt.
  Nicholson, Grover C. Jr., 2nd Lt.
  Wilson, Thomas P., WOJG (W-1)

Co. B, NCNG, Warrenton, N. C. (Federally Recognized 15 March 1947)

  Arrington, Samuel T., Captain
  Stallings, John W., 1st Lt.
  Floyd, Arthur H., WOJG (W-1)

Co. C, NCNG, Henderson, N. C. (Federally Recognized 17 July 1947)

  Cooper, Scott P., Captain
  Barnes, Floyd B., 1st Lt.
  Garrett, Herbert M., 2nd Lt.
  Pridgen, Benjamin M., 2nd Lt.

REPORT OF THE ADJUTANT GENERAL   113

Co. D, NCNG, Durham, N. C. (Federally Recognized 29 March 1948)
    Pendergrass, Coye L., Captain
    Durham, Robert J., 1st Lt.
    Beck, Robert V., 2nd Lt.
    Christmas, Edward L. Jr., 2nd Lt.
    Eakes, Joe O. Jr., 2nd Lt.
    Weiss, Joseph P., WOJG (W-1)

Hq Hq Co., 2nd Bn., NCNG, Wilson, N. C. (Federally Recognized 29 April 1947)
    Banzet, Frank B., Lt. Colonel
    Thompson, Lonnie F., Major
    Winstead, Edward J., Major
    Naugher, Loran D., Captain
    Seay, Raleigh F., Captain
    Stainback, Everett S. Jr., Captain
    Cook, Richard A., 1st Lt.
    Corrington, Ronald E. Jr., 2nd Lt.
    Newton, James E., 2nd Lt.
    Owens, Kirby C., 2nd Lt.
    Ives, Lowell W., WOJG (W-1)

Co. E, NCNG, Roanoke Rapids, N. C. (Federally Recognized 18 July 1947)
    Humphreys, Milton, 1st Lt.
    Waters, Admiral D. Jr., 1st Lt.
    Chestnut, Donald D., 2nd Lt.
    Hale, Joseph L., 2nd Lt.
    Peoples, Carl E., WOJG (W-1)

Co. F, NCNG, Tarboro, N. C. (Federally Recognized 9 July 1947)
    Smith, Oscar L., Captain
    Lockhart, Charles H., 1st Lt.
    Bailey, John J. Jr., 2nd Lt.
    Gardner, Walter M., WOJG (W-1)

Co. G, NCNG, Rocky Mount, N. C. (Federally Recognized 7 December 1948)
    Hertzberz, Sol, Captain
    Cuthrell, Hiram J., 1st Lt.
    Eaves, Charles T., 1st Lt.
    DeBow, Clyde E., 2nd Lt.
    Stephenson, Harold L., 2nd Lt.
    Pittman, Jasper L., WOJG (W-1)

Co. H., NCNG, Scotland Neck, N. C. (Federally Recognized 22 November 1948)
    Monroe, Orville N., Jr., 1st Lt.
    Allsbrook, David A., 2nd Lt.
    Edwards, Harold B., 2nd Lt.
    Allmond, William E. Jr., WOJG (W-1)

Hq Hq Co, 3rd Bn, NCNG, Clinton, N. C. (Federally Recognized 31 May 1948)
  Hughes, Robert A., Lt. Colonel
  Buck, William M., Major
  Eason, William L., Major
  Grissom, Robert M., Captain
  Kerr, Langdon C. Jr., Captain
  Summerlin, Charles A. Jr., Captain
  Shaw, William B., 1st Lt.
  Strickland, James F., 1st Lt.
  Tart, Clarence C. Jr., 1st Lt.
  Starling, William L. Jr., 2nd Lt.
  Bass, Willie C. Jr., WOJG (W-1)

Co. I, NCNG, Wilmington, N. C. (Federally Recognized 13 May 1947)
  MacDonald, Thomas H., Captain
  Morst, James H., 1st Lt.
  Rich, George T., 1st Lt.
  Milton, Hugh M., 2nd Lt.
  Strickland, James T., WOJG (W-1)

Co. K, NCNG, Fayetteville, N. C. (Federally Recognized 13 August 1948)
  Sanford, James T., Captain
  Beard, Wilbur F., 1st Lt.
  Armour, Franklin G., 2nd Lt.
  Marsh, Arthur, 2nd Lt.
  Millard, Junius H., 2nd Lt.
  Stahl, Wallace R., WOJG (W-1)

Co. L, NCNG, Goldsboro, N. C. (Federally Recognized 14 May 1947)
  Kannan, James C. Jr., Captain
  Crawford, Edward B., 1st Lt.
  Whitfield, Richard A., 1st Lt.
  Goff, James R., 2nd Lt.
  Starr, George E., WOJG (W-1)

Co. M, NCNG, Warsaw, N. C. ((Federally Recognized 14 April 1947)
  Merritt, Henry C., 1st Lt.
  Miller, James F., 1st Lt.
  Hasty, Rudolph F., 2nd Lt.
  Huie, Earl B., 2nd Lt.
  Whitfield, William B., WOJG (W-1)

120th Infantry

Hq Hq Co, NCNG, Reidsville, N. C. (Federally Recognized 22 April 1947)
  Parham, Maston S., Colonel
  Krueger, Warren R., Major
  Rogers, Duncan C. Jr., Major
  Summey, Thomas A. Jr., Major

Fitzgerald, Paul V. Jr., Captain
Meador, James R., Captain
Pooley, Robert C. Jr., Captain
Walker, Julius B., Captain
Barrow, Edward F., 1st Lt.
Groff, John J., 1st Lt.
Grogan, Earl M., 1st Lt.
Scott, Samuel F. Jr., 1st Lt.
Walker, Malcolm F., 1st Lt.
Bennett, Earnest A. Jr., 2nd Lt.
Gregory, Joseph F., 2nd Lt.
Robertson, Leonard T., 2nd Lt.
Vawter, Walter R. Jr., 2nd Lt.
Grogan, John W., CWO (W-2)
Thompson, Roy A., WOJG (W-1)

Service Co, NCNG, Asheville, N. C. (Federally Recognized 3 June 1947)

Abernethy, Leroy F. Jr., Major
Frady, Daniel W., Captain
Porter, Roswell K., Captain
Israel, William H., 2nd Lt.
Martin, Woodrow B., CWO (W-3)
Cundiff, Louis M. Jr., WOJG (W-1)
Drake, Robert E. Sr., WOJG (W-1)
Wilkinson, Ernest D. Jr., WOJG (W-1)
Yarborough, Lonnie P., WOJG (W-1)

Hv. Mortar Co., NCNG, Leaksville, N. C. (Federally Recognized 22 September 1947)

Dunton, Benjamin F., Captain
Riley, Rupert, 1st Lt.
Simpson, Jack P., 1st Lt.
Strother, William R., 1st Lt.
Gillespie, James A., 2nd Lt.
Brown, Lester N., WOJG (W-1)

Med. Tank Co, NCNG, Waynesville, N. C. (Federally Recognized 30 April 1947)

Carswell, Samuel A., Captain
Byrd, Frank C., 1st Lt.
Winchester, Robert H., 1st Lt.
Jones, Albert C., 2nd Lt.

Medical Co, NCNG, Mocksville, N. C. (Federally Recognized 29 September 1947)

Davis, Cornelius C., Captain
Lagle, Hugh A., Captain
Dickinson, Edgar C., 1st Lt.
Hendricks, Worth T., 1st Lt.
Sheek, James K. Jr., 1st Lt.

Hq Hq Co, 1st Bn, NCNG, Mt. Airy, N. C. (Federally Recognized 16 March 1948)

    Sutton, Albert D., Lt. Colonel
    Hayes, James M. Jr., Major
    Hudson, James G., Major
    Baker, Ruggles L., Captain
    Davis, John C., Captain
    Einstein, Frederick M. Jr., Captain
    Jones, Kenneth K. Jr., 2nd Lt.
    McNeil, James R., WOJG (W-1)

Co. A, NCNG, Burlington, N. C. (Federally Recognized 20 August 1947)

    Davis, David F., Captain
    Bradshaw, Thomas S., 1st Lt.
    McDonald, James D., 1st Lt.
    Pickard, Marvin C., 1st Lt.
    Hinshaw, Arned, 2nd Lt.
    Gibson, Reginald T., WOJG (W-1)

Co. B, NCNG, Winston-Salem, N. C. (Federally Recognized 15 October 1947)

    Blalock, Conrad M., Captain
    Kelly, Jack T., 1st Lt.
    Keller, William R. Sr., 2nd Lt.
    Kennington, Lloyd H., 2nd Lt.
    Stoneman, James N., 2nd Lt.
    Holcomb, Weldon E., WOJG (W-1)

Co. C, NCNG, Lexington, N. C. (Federally Recognized 22 January 1948)

    Barnes, Beamer H., Captain
    Brooks, Judson L., 1st Lt.
    Farmer, Lewis J., 1st Lt.
    Foster, James R., 1st Lt.
    Honeycutt, Lester V., 1st Lt.

Co. D, NCNG, Winston-Salem, N. C. (Federally Recognized 6 August 1947)

    Robinson, James M., Captain
    Hutchins, Willie L., 1st Lt.
    Talbert, Russell L., Jr., 1st Lt.
    Hinshaw, James T. Jr., 2nd Lt.

Hq Hq Co, 2nd Bn, NCNG, Asheboro, N. C. (Federally Recognized 6 January 1948)

    Presnell, Tom, Lt. Colonel
    Lambeth, Benjamin F., Captain
    Morris, Eugene T., Captain
    Taylor, Albert G., Captain

REPORT OF THE ADJUTANT GENERAL 117

>Wall, Alton P. Captain
>Cox, Hobart C., 1st Lt.
>Steed, Lawrence L., 1st Lt.
>Redding, Ray E., 2nd Lt.
>Toler, Frank G. Jr., 2nd Lt.
>Rich, Charles H., WOJG (W-1)

Co. E, NCNG, Concord, N. C. (Federally Recognized 13 March 1947)
>Robbins, Eugene A. Jr., Captain
>Belo, Harry L., 1st Lt.
>Ferguson, Edwin H., 1st Lt.
>Nance, Walter L., 1st Lt.
>Smith, Roddy L., 1st Lt.
>Williams, Robert O., 2nd Lt.

Co. F, NCNG, Albemarle, N. C. (Federally Recognized 12 September 1947)
>Rudisill, Gerald A., Captain
>Beck, Donald A., 1st Lt.
>Love, Adam W., 1st Lt.
>Melton, Joe Z., 2nd Lt.
>Thomas, Benjamin F., 2nd Lt.
>Pegram, Walter W., WOJG (W-1)

Co. G, NCNG, Salisbury, N. C. (Federally Recognized 27 June 1947)
>Murdoch, William S., Captain
>Bradshaw, Arthur L., 2nd Lt.
>Clark, Earnest A., 2nd Lt.
>Leonard, Donald L., 2nd Lt.

Co. H, NCNG, Hickory, N. C. (Federally Recognized 14 March 1947)
>VanderLinden, William H. Jr., Captain
>Beach, Aaron L., 1st Lt.
>Brown, Van H., 1st Lt.

Hq Hq Co, 3rd Bn, NCNG, Kings Mountains, N. C. (Federally Recognized 16 June 1948)
>Davis, James M., Lt. Colonel
>Bolin, Banks E., Major
>Burrell, Ray G., Captain
>Cash, Paul S., Captain
>Houston, Samuel H., Captain
>Malony, James L., Captain
>Stegall, Harry E. Jr., 2nd Lt.
>Stegall, Robert L., 2nd Lt.
>Gantt, Ned L., WOJG (W-1)

Co. I, NCNG, Newton, N. C. (Federally Recognized 23 April 1947)
>Wanzer, Charles R., Captain
>Barringer, Jack E., 1st Lt.
>Taylor, William E., 1st Lt.
>Lambeth, Donald C., 2nd Lt.

Co. K, NCNG, Gastonia, N. C. (Federally Recognized 24 July 1947)
    Harris, William F., Captain
    Armstrong, William B., 1st Lt.
    Barham, Jackson T., 1st Lt.
    Dover, Harvey L., 1st Lt.
    Ratchford, Charles N., 2nd Lt.

Co. L, NCNG, Morganton, N. C. (Federally Recognized 14 July 1947)
    Bigham, Robert W., 1st Lt.
    Walker, Charles W., 1st Lt.
    Wiltshire, John L., 1st Lt.
    Baker, Frank M., 2nd Lt.

Co. M, NCNG, Morganton, N. C. (Federally Recognized 10 March 1947)
    Cabaniss, Robert E., Captain
    Scoggins, William C. Jr., 1st Lt.
    Weir, William H., 1st Lt.

112th FA Bn

Hq Hq Btry, NCNG, Lenoir, N. C. (Federally Recognized 9 June 1947)
    Thompson, Roy E., Lt. Colonel
    Biggerstaff, Charles W., Major
    Forehand, Roy W., Major
    Carpenter, Howard G., Captain
    Rader, Ervin D., Captain
    Smith, Boone E., Captain
    Smith, Hal H., Captain
    Tuttle, Robert H., Captain
    Underdown, Sidney L., Captain
    Hartley, Harold W., 1st Lt.
    Robbins, Lawrence N., 1st Lt.
    Swanson, Garland W., 1st Lt.
    Silver, Leon S., 2nd Lt.
    Walker, Newland E., 2nd Lt.
    Beach, James W., WOJG (W-1)

Service Btry, NCNG, Lenoir, N. C. (Federally Recognized 26 October 1948)
    Seehorn, Theodore R., Captain
    Beach, Darwin E., 1st Lt.
    Morgan, Raymond L., 1st Lt.
    Harless, James C., CWO (W-2)
    Rhodes, Lloyd G., WOJG (W-1)

Btry A, NCNG, Forest City, N. C. (Federally Recognized 14 November 1947)
    Bradley, Grover H., Captain
    Kichinko, Michael N. III, 1st Lt.
    Peeler, William B., 2nd Lt.
    Vess, Gudger G., WOJG (W-1)

REPORT OF THE ADJUTANT GENERAL 119

Btry B, NCNG, Spindale, N. C. (Federally Recognized 13 November 1947)

    Green, Herman E., Captain
    Padgett, Max, 1st Lt.
    Poteat, George W., 1st Lt.
    Wilkie, Hubert G., 1st Lt.
    Harper, Fred R., WOJG (W-1)

Btry C, NCNG, North Wilkesboro, N. C. (Federally Recognized 3 February 1948)

    Boldin, Ralph A., Captain
    Faw, Claude C., Jr., 1st Lt.
    Thomas, William S. Jr., 1st Lt.
    Wiles, Clarence D., 2nd Lt.

113th FA Bn

Hq Hq Btry, NCNG, Louisburg, N. C. (Federally Recognized 28 August 1947)

    Perry, Darrell L., Major
    Yarborough, Edward F., Major
    Daniel, Justice G., Captain
    Denning, James W., Captain
    Duncan, Roland F., Captain
    Holmes, Melvin C., Captain
    McKinne, Collin, Captain
    Pearce, Philip D., Captain
    Griffin, William S. Jr., 1st Lt.
    Fuller, Kenneth A., 2nd Lt.
    Redmond, Franklin P., 2nd Lt.
    Stewart, Paul W., 2nd Lt.
    Morton, Willard D., CWO (W-2)
    Johnson, James A., WOJG (W-1)

Service Btry, NCNG, Youngsville, N. C. (Federally Recognized 18 August 1947)

    Brown, Wiley, 1st Lt.
    Dickens, Lucius H. II, 2nd Lt.
    Wall, Oliver W., 2nd Lt.
    Cheatham, Robert E., CWO (W-3)

Btry A, NCNG, Zebulon, N. C. ((Federally Recognized 27 July 1949)

    'Davis, Barrie S., Captain
    Hinds, George H., 1st Lt.
    Finch, Foster D. Jr., 2nd Lt.
    Potter, James M., Jr., 2nd Lt.

Btry B, NCNG, Dunn, N. C. (Federally Recognized 10 November 1947)
>   Blalock, George F., Captain
>   Duncan, George W., 2nd Lt.
>   Hall, Francis W., 2nd Lt.
>   Wade, Edward H., 2nd Lt.
>   Lee, James N., WOJG (W-1)

Btry C, NCNG, Roxboro, N. C. (Federally Recognized 9 April 1948)
>   Yeaman, James G., Captain
>   Wright, Wallace L., 1st Lt.
>   Hicks, Willie B., 2nd Lt.
>   Gentry, Ollie P., WOJG (W-1)

130th AAA AW Bn

Hq Hq Btry, NCNG, Red Springs, N. C. (Federally Recognized 10 June 1947)
>   Lamont, William Jr., Lt. Colonel
>   Dickson, Paul, Major
>   Lester, Thomas B. Jr., Major
>   Bullock, Walter R., Captain
>   McLean, Herbert S. Jr., Captain
>   McMillan, Harvey F., 1st Lt.
>   Brock, Jimmy W., 2nd Lt.
>   Sighel, Norman C., CWO (W-2)
>   McMillan, Charles P., WOJG (W-1)

Btry A, NCNG, Raeford, N. C. (Federally Recognized 10 March 1947)
>   English, Talmadge, 1st Lt.
>   Newton, Edwin D., 1st Lt.
>   Poole, William L. Jr., 1st Lt.
>   Macko, Thomas M., 2nd Lt.
>   Dixon, Roger W., WOJG (W-1)

Btry B, NCNG, St. Pauls, N. C. (Federally Recognized 8 November 1949)
>   Powers, Russell H., Captain
>   Musselwhite, James C., 2nd Lt.
>   Sugar, Stanly, 2nd Lt.
>   Sherrill, Joe E. Jr., WOJG (W-1)

Btry C, NCNG, Sanford, N. C. (Federally Recognized 11 June 1948)
>   Staton, William W., Captain
>   Smith, Billie C., 1st Lt.
>   Winders, Gilbert L. Jr., 1st Lt.
>   McDonald, Thomas W., WOJG (W-1)

Btry D, NCNG, Southern Pines, N. C. (Federally Recognized 7 October 1949)
>   Wilson, William J., Captain
>   Irvin, James L., 1st Lt.
>   Horner, Ralph L., 2nd Lt.
>   Forsyth, Lennox, WOJG (W-1)

(NON-DIV)

IV Corps Arty, NCNG, Charlotte, N. C. (Federally Recognized 9 October 1950)

    Guthrie, Kermit L., Lt. Colonel
    Purvis, John A., Lt. Colonel
    St. George, William M., Major
    Byrum, Porter B., Captain
    Ewing, William C., Captain
    Friddle, George H., Captain
    Garland, James B., Captain
    Gibbs, Wallace D. Jr., Captain
    Isom, Charles D. Jr., Captain
    Manning, James T. Jr., Captain
    Cooper, George W., 1st Lt.
    Haubenrieser, Robert J., 1st Lt.
    Kirkman, Guilford M., 1st Lt.
    Shaw, Victor Jr., 1st Lt.
    Connor, James W., 2nd Lt.
    Huggins, Jimmie B., 2nd Lt.
    Huggins, John S., 2nd Lt.
    Morse, Harris A., WOJG (W-1)

196th FA Group, NCNG, Kinston, N. C. (Federally Recognized 26 August 1948)

    Willis, Weston H., Colonel
    Kornegay, Joseph T., Major
    Langston, Guy C., Major
    Bell, Richard K., Captain
    Dupree, Louis J. Jr., Captain
    Glover, Murrell K., Captain
    Simmons, Thomas W., Captain
    Thompson, Robert L. Jr., Captain
    Ward, Clement M. Jr., Captain
    Quinn, Horace R., 1st Lt.
    Thompson, William M., 1st Lt.
    Waters, William G. Jr., 1st Lt.
    Crary, Earnest F., CWO (W-4)
    Bourdas, Alexander, WOJG (W-1)
    McLawhorn, Charles H., WOJG (W-1)
    Sugg, Charles F., WOJG (W-1)

252nd AAA Group, NCNG, Wilmington, N. C. (Federally Recognized 10 February 1948)

    Corbett, Kenneth M., Colonel
    Cobb, William A., Lt. Colonel
    Boylan, Joseph E. Jr., Major
    Brown, Michael C., Major
    Farmer, John E., Major
    Reid, Henry V., Major

Morris, Cliff C. Jr., Captain
Primrose, Hugh W., Captain
Smith, Arthur T., Captain
Walls, Osborne K., Captain
Bowden, Laurence O., 2nd Lt.
Crabtree, Purvis G., 2nd Lt.
Herring, Oscar C., 2nd Lt.
Lanier, Homer A., 2nd Lt.
Orrell, Ernest C., CWO (W-2)
Buck, Robert B., WOJG (W-1)
Jeb Lee, John P. Jr., WOJG (W-1)
King, Adolph L. Jr., WOJG (W-1)
Proctor, Grady M., WOJG (W-1)
Williams, Russell C. Jr., WOJG (W-1)

725th AAA AW Bn

Hq Hq Btry, NCNG, Whiteville, N. C. (Federally Recognized 10 January 1950)

Bowles, David A., Major
Maultsby, John C., Major
Brooks, James A., Captain
Burns, John K., Captain
Maultsby, Alexander, Captain
Powell, Walter H. Jr., Captain
Waldron, Harold A., Captain
Dickens, Wallace J., 1st Lt.
Hickman, James B., 1st Lt.
Maxwell, James R., 1st Lt.
Chesnutt, Norwood B. Jr., 2nd Lt.
Rooks, Robert O., CWO (W-4)
FormyDuval, John M., WOJG (W-1)

Btry A, NCNG, Shallotte, N. C. (Federally Recognized 28 November 1949)

Carmichael, David B., 1st Lt.
Holden, Kemp R., 1st Lt.
Sellers, William T., 1st Lt.

Btry B, NCNG, Fair Bluff, N. C. (Federally Recognized 1 May 1950)

Enzor, Simeon T., Captain
Scott, Jimmie A., 1st Lt.
Collins, Lawrence O., 2nd Lt.
Rogers, Ed F. Jr., WOJG (W-1)

Btry C, NCNG, Bladenboro, N. C. (Federally Recognized 17 January 1950)

Britt, David L., Captain
Bullard, Johnnie G., 2nd Lt.
Cook, Andrew G., 2nd Lt.
Stevens, Bennie E., 2nd Lt.

252nd FA Group, NCNG, Greensboro, N. C. (Federally Recognized 2 November 1950)

    Wrenn, Oscar I., Colonel
    Brown, Thomas E., Lt. Colonel
    Compton, Carl S., Major
    Taylor, Raleigh C. Jr., Major
    Wannamaker, Charles W. Jr., Major
    Carlton, Philip R. Jr., Captain
    Groome, William A., Captain
    Lewis, Radford F., Captain
    McGinnis, James W. (Chaplain) Captain
    King, Hurley D., 1st Lt.
    East, Larry E., 2nd Lt.
    Jones, George S., CWO (W-3)

505th FA Bn

Hq Hq Btry, NCNG, Greensboro, N. C. (Federally Recognized 20 April 1947)

    Carruthers, Joseph T. Jr., Lt. Colonel
    Brandt, Leon J. Jr., Major
    Ballard, William M. Jr., Captain
    Gerringer, Linley W. Jr., Captain
    Mitchell, Fillmore I., Jr., Captain
    Williams, Hugh B., Captain
    Mathews, Joseph A., 1st Lt.
    Mullis, John B., 1st Lt.
    Cates, John B., WOJG (W-1)

Service Btry, NCNG, Greensboro, N. C. (Federally Recognized 2 December 1948)

    Hanner, George K., Captain
    Smith, Clarence D., 1st Lt.
    Bateman, Robert M., CWO (W-2)

Med Det, NCNG, Greensboro, N. C. (Federally Recognized 24 October 1949)

    Reid, William J., Captain

Btry A, NCNG, Greensboro, N. C. (Federally Recognized 8 July 1948)

    Root, Hardy S., Captain
    Lewis, Richard W., 2nd Lt.
    Pinnix, James C., 2nd Lt.
    Tesh, Robert L., WOJG (W-1)

Btry B, NCNG, Greensboro, N. C. (Federally Recognized 11 October 1949)

    Gibson, Belton H. Jr., Captain
    Faison, Gaston D., 1st Lt.
    Lewis, Kenneth E., 2nd Lt.
    Yow, Clarence L., WOJG (W-1)

124   REPORT OF THE ADJUTANT GENERAL

Btry C, NCNG, Greensboro, N. C. (Federally Recognized 17 November 1950)

    Poole, Frank R. Jr., Captain
    Chalmers, Carl M., 1st Lt.
    Fox, William D., 2nd Lt.

167th MP Bn

Hq Hq Co, NCNG, Ahoskie, N. C. (Federally Recognized 26 February 1951)

    Peterson, Bernice A., Lt. Colonel
    Modlin, Morton S., Major
    Blythe, Joseph D., Captain
    Beale, Walter H. Jr., 1st Lt.
    Bennett, Columbus L., 1st Lt.
    Best, Edward P., 2nd Lt.
    McBryde, Everett L., 2nd Lt.
    Bennett, Robert A., WOJG (W-1)
    Holloman, Elmo H., WOJG (W-1)
    Pierce, John N., WOJG (W-1)
    Smith, Harry L., WOJG, (W-1)

Co. A, NCNG, Windsor, N. C. (Federally Recognized 26 February 1951)

    Spruill, Charles B., Captain
    Pierce, Melvin E., 2nd Lt.
    Stanley, Howard T., 2nd Lt.

123rd Signal Radar Maint. Unit, Type C, NCNG, Wilmington, N. C. (Federally Recognized 24 January 1951)

    Casey, Jephthah Jr., WOJG (W-1)

217th RCAT Det, NCNG, Raleigh, N. C. (Federally Recognized 7 February 1951)

    Smith, Kerr H., 2nd Lt.

94th Army Band, NCNG, Raleigh, N. C. (Federally Recognized 24 February 1947)

    Burt, Millard P., CWO (W-3)

3624th Ord Med Maint Co, NCNG, Butner, N. C. (Federally Recognized 20 February 1948)

    Davis, Louis H., 1st Lt.
    Fletcher, James M., 1st Lt.
    Kubachko, Andrew Jr., 1st Lt.
    Gay, George A., 2nd Lt.
    Ferrell, Arthur E., CWO (W-2)
    Lemons, Arthur L., WOJG (W-1)

121st AAA Operations Det., NCNG, Charlotte, N. C. (Federally Recognized 14 Dec 1951)

    Boone, Benjamin K., Major
    Sproles, James W., 1st Lt.

AIR UNITS

Hq, NC ANG, Charlotte, N. C.

    Coleman, Robert W., Lt. Colonel
    Brooks, Robert W. Jr., Major
    Higgins, Robert G., Major
    Harding, Frederic D., Captain

8156th Air Base Sq. NCANG, Charlotte, N. C.

    Shelden, Howard W., 1st Lt.

ROSTER OF OFFICERS AND WARRANT OFFICERS IN THE NORTH CAROLINA NATIONAL GUARD AS OF 31 DECEMBER 1952

ARMY UNITS
(NON-DIV)

Hq Hq Det, NC NG, Raleigh, N. C. (Federally Recognized 18 March 1947)

    Austell, Michael H., Colonel
    Jonas, Charles R., Colonel
    Upton, Thomas H., Colonel
    Broaddus, Russell G., Lt. Colonel
    Bruton, Thomas W., Lt. Colonel
    Cavaness, Hugh L., Lt. Colonel
    Edwards, Daniel K., Lt. Colonel
    Foreman, John, Lt. Colonel
    Hutchinson, Henry H., Lt. Colonel
    Pickens, Wiley M., Lt. Colonel
    Armstrong, Lee Roy W., Major
    Avery, Isaac T. Jr., Major
    Brown, Thomas C., Major
    Donovan, David W., Major
    Leinster, Joseph A., Major
    Ludwig, Edward W., Major
    Mathis, Quince E., Major
    Pait, Neil J. Jr., Major
    Ratchford, Charles B., Major
    Reitzel, John L., Major
    Davis, James F., Captain
    Lewis, Walter C., Captain
    Wilkins, Robert J., Captain
    York, Richard G., Captain
    Carter, Thomas E., 1st Lt.
    Hayes, Grayson, 1st Lt.
    Massengill, Hugh P., 1st Lt.
    Sechriest, Stuart W., 1st Lt.
    Byerly, Armitt B., WOJG (W-2)
    Patrick, William L., WOJG (W-1))

(DIV-UNITS)

Hq 30th Inf Div (In Part), NCNG, Raleigh, N. C. (Federally Recognized 11 Sept 1947)

    Bowers, Claude T., Brig. General
    Davis, Fitzgerald E., Lt. Colonel
    Lee, Joel T., Lt. Colonel
    Longest, Thomas B., Lt. Colonel
    Manning, Howard E., Lt. Colonel
    Shimer, Clarence B., Lt. Colonel
    Blalock, George F., Major
    Currin, Robert G., Major

Davis, Ferd L., Major
Manooch, Charles S. Jr., Major
Patterson, Eugene R., Major
Smith, Kenneth A., Major
Stott, Charles C., Major
Vinson, James A., Major
Alford, Lonnie R., Captain
Coxe, James S. Jr., Captain
Holoman, William K., Captain
Shelden, Robert E. H., Captain
Clark, Luther W., 1st Lt.
Liles, Graydon C., 1st Lt.
Marks, Charles L., 1st Lt.
Robinson, Bernard E., 1st Lt.
Gminder, Russell, 2nd Lt.
Outlaw, Jennings C., 2nd Lt.
Jones, Donald B., WOJG (W-1)
Link, Wallace G., WOJG (W-1)
Oglesby, Thomas B., WOJG (W-1)
Pate, Chester E., WOJG (W-1)

Hq Co 30th Inf Div (Less Separate Det), NCNG, Apex, N. C. (Federally Recognized 22 March 1948)

Ashley, Jay L., Captain
Edwards, Everette M. Jr., 2nd Lt.
King, Centennial C., 2nd Lt.
Snotherly, Henry A., 2nd Lt.
Riley, Fred T., WOJG (W-1)

Sep. Det. Hq. Co. 30th Inf Div NCNG, Raleigh-Durham Airport. (Federally Recognized 22 March 1948)

Bass, Mack G. Jr., Captain
Gay, George A., 1st Lt.
Hutchins, James T., 1st Lt.
Elliott, Leighton M., 2nd Lt.
Pulley, James F., Jr., 2nd Lt.

Med Det 30th Inf Div NCNG, Apex, N. C. (Federally Recognized 13 January 1950)

Hart, Lillard, F., Major

Signal Co., NCNG, Canton, N. C. (Federally Recognized 14 May 1947)

Blalock, Clifton E. Jr., Major
Chapman, Weaver C., Captain
Cooper, Woodrow W., Captain
Keylon, Arthur F., 1st Lt.
Smathers, Sigmon W., 1st Lt.
White, James A., 1st Lt.
Russell, Jack H., 2nd Lt.
Davis, Stuart M., WOJG (W-1)
Johnson, Charles S., WOJG (W-1)

REPORT OF THE ADJUTANT GENERAL

119th Infantry

   Hq Hq Co, NCNG, Durham, N. C. (Federally Recognized 8 July 1947)

      Hardesty, Ivan, Colonel
      Banzet, Frank B., Lt. Colonel
      Cartwright, John W., Major
      Harrison, George W., Major
      Sanders, Richard T., Major
      Lougee, Henry S., Captain
      McGinnis, James W., Captain
      Pennington, Hubert E., Captain
      Pickett, Stewart M., Captain
      White-Hurst, Bernard, Captain
      Cleveland, Robert, 1st Lt.
      Raynor, George E. Jr., 1st Lt.
      Hale, Claude E. Jr., 1st Lt.
      Scott, Jesse P., 1st Lt.
      Coggin, John R. Jr., 2nd Lt.
      Mansfield, Raymond, 2nd Lt.
      Milton, Hugh M., 2nd Lt.
      Veasey, Sterling S. Jr., 2nd Lt.
      Rees, Leland M., WOJG (W-1)

   Medical Co, NCNG, Wilson, N. C. (Federally Recognized 10 March 1949)

      Hood, John M., Captain
      Taylor, Allen, Captain
      Boyette, Earl R., 2nd Lt.
      Grady, Paul D., 2nd Lt.
      Lamm, John G., 2nd Lt.
      Smiley, Melvin W., 2nd Lt.
      Vick, George C. Jr., 2nd Lt.

   Service Co, NCNG, Elizabeth City, N. C. (Federally Recognized 8 April 1947)

      Ingram, William E., Major
      Scott, Shelton G., Captain
      White, Beverly W., Captain.
      Harrell, Benjamin C., 2nd Lt.
      Chapin, William McC., CWO (W-2)
      Hill, Joseph E., CWO (W-2)
      Helmkamp, Richard C., WOJG (W-1)
      Warren, Gerald R., WOJG (W-1)

   Hv Mortar Co, NCNG, Edenton, N. C. (Federally Recognized 12 May 1947)

      Fry, Cecil W., Captain
      Swanner, Charlie W., 1st Lt.
      Moore, Wayland C. Jr., 2nd Lt.
      Swanner, Joseph K., 2nd Lt.
      Asbell, John H. Jr., WOJG (W-1)

REPORT OF THE ADJUTANT GENERAL   129

Med Tank Co, NCNG, Parkton, N. C. (Federally Recognized 16 September 1947)
 Hall, Roger F., Captain
 Acree, Carl F., 1st Lt.
 Smathers, Rufus E., 1st Lt.
 Stalling, John W., 1st Lt.
 McGougan, Ernest D., 2nd Lt.
 Hall, James E. Jr., WOJG (W-1)

Hq Hq Co 1st Bn, NCNG, Durham, N. C. (Federally Recognized 3 October 1947))
 Steagall, Gordon I., Lt. Colonel
 Floyd, John E., Major
 Sanders, Harper K. Jr., Major
 Barnes, Lee R., Captain
 Bouchard, Arthur J., Captain
 Durham, Robert J., Captain
 Keeton, William P. Jr., Captain
 Chandler, Malcolm T., 1st Lt.
 Dennis, Luther A., 2nd Lt.
 Dudley, Roland E., 2nd Lt.
 Pickett, Claudius A., 2nd Lt.

Co. A, NCNG, Oxford, N. C. (Federally Recognized 12 May 1947)
 Hancock, Franklin W., III, 1st Lt.
 Nicholson, Grover C. Jr., 1st Lt.
 Puckett, Hoyle B., 1st Lt.
 Tenhet, Joseph N. Jr., 1st Lt.
 Wilson, Thomas P., WOJG (W-1)

Co. B, NCNG, Warrenton, N. C. (Federally Recognized 15 Mar 1947)
 Arrington, Samuel T., Captain
 Eaves, Charles T., 1st Lt.
 Collins, Leland M., 2nd Lt.
 Currie, Roger L., 2nd Lt.
 Evans, Thomas M., 2nd Lt.
 Powell, Thomas H., 2nd Lt.
 Floyd, Arthur H., WOJG (W-1)

Co. C, NCNG, Henderson, N. C. (Federally Recognized 19 July 1947)
 Cooper, Scott P., Captain
 Barnes, Floyd P., 1st Lt.
 Garrett, Herbert M., 1st Lt.
 Pridgen, Benjamin M., 1st Lt.
 Tucker, George N. Jr., 2nd Lt.
 Faulkner, Durwood W., WOJG (W-1)

Co. D, NCNG, Durham, N. C. (Federally Recognized 29 March 1948)
 Pendergrass, Coye L., Captain
 Christmas, Edward L. Jr., 2nd Lt.

Eakes, Joe O. Jr., 2nd Lt.
Jary, Bernard J., 2nd Lt.
Newton, Walter C. Jr., 2nd Lt.
Weiss, Joseph P., WOJG (W-1)

Hq. Hq. 2nd Bn, NCNG, Wilson, N. C. (Federally Recognized 29 April 1947)

Taylor, Herbert H. Jr., Lt. Colonel
Naugher, Loran D., Major
Winstead, Edward J., Major
Hertzberg, Sol., Captain
Stainback, Everett S. Jr., Captain
Cook, Richard A., 1st Lt.
Corrington, Ronald E. Jr., 2nd Lt.
Newton, James E., 2nd Lt.
Owens, Kirby C., 2nd Lt.
Ives, Lowell W., WOJG (W-1)

Co. E, NCNG, Roanoke Rapids, N. C. (Federally Recognized 18 July 1947)

Hale, Joseph L., 1st Lt.
Humphreys, Milton, 1st Lt.
Waters, Admiral D. Jr., 1st Lt.
Hockaday, Alvin T., 2nd Lt.
Peoples, Carl E., WOJG (W-1)

Co. F, NCNG, Tarboro, N. C. (Federally Recognized 9 July 1947)

Smith, Oscar L., Captain
Brock, Linwood M., 1st Lt.
Lockhart, Charles H., 1st Lt.
Bailey, John J. Jr., 2nd Lt.
Gardner, Walter M., WOJG (W-1)

Co. G, NCNG, Rocky Mount, N. C. (Federally Recognized 7 December 1948)

Cuthrell, Hiram J., 1st Lt.
DeBow, Clyde E., 2nd Lt.
Reid, James W. Jr., 2nd Lt.
Stephenson, Harold L., 2nd Lt.
Pittman, Jasper L., WOJG (W-1)

Co. H, NCNG, Scotland Neck, N. C. (Federally Recognized 22 November 1948)

Monroe, Orville N. J., Captain
Allsbrook, David A., 2nd Lt.
Allmond, William E. Jr., WOJG (W-1)

Hq Hq 3rd Bn, NCNG, Clinton, N. C. (Federally Recognized 31 May 1948)

Hughes, Robert A., Lt. Colonel
Buck, William M., Major
Eason, William L., Major

REPORT OF THE ADJUTANT GENERAL 131

    Grissom, Robert M., Captain
    MacDonald, Thomas H., Captain
    Shaw, William B., Captain
    Summerlin, Charles A., Captain
    Strickland, James F., 1st Lt.
    Hasty, Rudolph F., 2nd Lt.
    Starling, William L. Jr., 2nd Lt.

Co. I, NCNG, Wilmington, N. C. (Federally Recognized 13 May 1947)

    Morse, James H. Captain
    Rich, George T., 1st Lt.
    Keen, Walter E. Jr., 2nd Lt.
    Waldoch, Donald J., 2nd Lt.
    Strickland, James T., WOJG (W-1)

Co. K, NCNG, Fayetteville, N. C. (Federally Recognized 13 August 1948)

    Sanford, James T., Captain
    Armour, Franklin G., 1st Lt.
    Beard, Wilbur F., 1st Lt.
    DeVane, James D. III, 1st Lt.
    West, John L., 1st Lt.
    Millard, Junius H., 2nd Lt.
    Stahl, Wallace R., WOJG (W-1)

Co. L, NCNG, Goldsboro, N. C. (Federally Recognized 14 May 1947)

    Kannan, James C. Jr., Captain
    Crawford, Edward B., 1st Lt.
    Whitfield, Richard A., 1st Lt.
    Goff, James R., 2nd Lt.
    Lashley, Eugene M., 2nd Lt.

Co. M, NCNG, Warsaw, N. C. (Federally Recognized 14 April 1947)

    Merritt, Henry C., Captain
    Huie, Earl B., 1st Lt.
    Allen, Harvey C. Jr., 2nd Lt.
    Kornegay, George C., 2nd Lt.
    Rivenbark, Raymond W., 2nd Lt.
    Whitfield, William B., WOJG (W-1)

120th Infantry

Hq Hq Co, NCNG, Reidsville, N. C. (Federally Recognized 22 April 1947)

    Parham, Maston S., Colonel
    Krueger, Warren R., Major
    Rogers, Duncan C. Jr., Major
    Summey, Thomas A. Jr., Major
    Davis, John C., Captain
    Fitzgerald, Paul V. Jr., Captain
    Meador, James R., Captain
    Walker, Julius B., Captain

Wilkinson, David E., Captain
Barroe, Edward F., 1st Lt.
Bennett, Earnest A. Jr., 1st Lt.
Gregory, Joseph F., 1st Lt.
Groff, John J., 1st Lt.
Grogan, Earl M., 1st Lt.
Robertson, Leonard T., 1st Lt.
Scott, Samuel F. Jr., 1st Lt.
Walker, Malcolm F., 1st Lt.
Grogan, John W., CWO (W-2)
Thompson, Roy A., WOJG (W-1)

Service Co, NCNG, Asheville, N. C. (Federally Recognized 3 June 1947)

Abernethy, Leroy F. Jr., Major
Frady, Daniel W., Captain
Porter, Roswell K., Captain
Israel, William H., 2nd Lt.
Martin, Woodrow B., CWO (W-2)

Hv. Mortar Co, NCNG, Leaksville, N. C. (Federally Recognized 22 September 1947)

Dunton, Benjamin F., Captain
Gillespie, James A., 1st Lt.
Riley, Rupert, 1st Lt.
Simpson, Jack P., 1st Lt.
Strother, Willam R., 1st Lt.
Brown, Lester N., WOJG (W-1)

Tank Co (90MM Gun), NCNG, Waynesville, N. C. (Federally Recognized 30 April 1947)

Carswell, Samuel A., Captain
Byrd, Frank C., 1st Lt.
Winchester, Robert H., 1st Lt.
Adams, James R., 2nd Lt.
Jones, Albert C., 2nd Lt.
Mull, Paul M., WOJG (W-1)

Medical Co, NCNG, Mocksville, N. C. (Federally Recognized 29 September 1947)

Lagle, Hugh A., Captain
Dickinson, Edgar C., 1st Lt.
Hendricks, Worth T., 1st Lt.
Latta, James E., 2nd Lt.

Hq Hq Co, 1st Bn, NCNG, Mt. Airy, N. C. (Federally Recognized 16 March 1948)

Sutton, Albert D., Lt. Colonel
Hayes, James M. Jr., Major
Hudson, James C., Major
Baker, Ruggles L., Captain

Barnes, Beamer H., Captain
Einstein, Frederick M. Jr., Captain
Jones, Kenneth K. Jr., 1st Lt.
Keller, William R. Sr., 1st Lt.
Bowman, Russell E., 2nd Lt.
McNeil, James R., WOJG

Co. A, NCNG, Burlington, N. C. (Federally Recognized 20 August 1947)

McDonald, James D., 1st Lt.
Pickard, Marvin C., 1st Lt.
Hinshaw, Arned, 2nd Lt.
Gibson, Reginald T., WOJG

Co. B, NCNG, Winston-Salem, N. C. (Federally Recognized 15 October 1947)

Blalock, Conrad M., Captain
Kelly, Jack T., 1st Lt.
Kennington, Lloyd H., 1st Lt.
Stoneman, James N., 2nd Lt.
Holcomb, Weldon E., WOJG

Co. C, NCNG, Lexington, N. C. (Federally Recognized 22 January 1948)

Honeycutt, Lester V., Captain
Farmer, Lewis J., 1st Lt.
Foster, James R., 1st Lt.
Jenkins, James L., WOJG

Co. D, NCNG, Winston-Salem, N. C. (Federally Recognized 6 August 1947)

Hutchins, Willie L., Captain
Hinshaw, James T. Jr., 1st Lt.
Talbert, Russell L. Jr., 1st Lt.

Hq Hq Co, 2nd Bn, NCNG, Asheboro, N. C. (Federally Recognized 6 January 1948)

Presnell, Tom, Lt. Colonel
Malony, James L., Captain
Morris, Eugene T., Captain
Rudisill, Gerald A., Captain
Taylor, Albert G., Captain
Wall, Alton P., Captain
Cox, Hobart C., 1st Lt.
Steed, Lawrence L., 1st Lt.
McBryde, Fred H. Jr., 2nd Lt.
Redding, Ray E., 2nd Lt.
Toler, Frank G. Jr., 2nd Lt.
Rich, Charles H., WOJG

Co. E, NCNG, Concord, N. C. (Federally Recognized 13 March 1947)
> Robbins, Eugene A. Jr., Captain
> Belo, Harry L., 1st Lt.
> Baltes, Harold W., 2nd Lt.
> Williams, Robert O., 2nd Lt.
> Smith, Robert W. Jr., WOJG

Co. F, NCNG, Albemarle, N. C. (Federally Recognized 12 September 1947)
> Beck, Donald A., 1st Lt.
> Garrison, John T., 1st Lt.
> Love, Adam W., 1st Lt.
> Melton, Joe Z., 1st Lt.
> Newman, John T. V., 2nd Lt.
> Pegram, Walter W., WOJG

Co. G, NCNG, Salisbury, N. C. (Federally Recognized 27 June 1947)
> Murdoch, William S., Captain
> Bradshaw, Arthur L., 2nd Lt.
> Clark, Ernest A., 2nd Lt.
> Lee, Robert E., 2nd Lt.
> Leonard, Donald L., 2nd Lt.

Co. H, NCNG, Hickory, N. C. (Federally Recognized 14 March 1947)
> Beach, Aaron L., 1st Lt.
> Edwards, Earl T. Jr., 1st Lt.

Hq Hq Co, 3rd Bn, NCNG, Kings Mountain, N. C. (Federally Recognized 16 June 1948)
> Davis, James M., Lt. Colonel
> Bolin, Banks E., Major
> Burrell, Ray G., Captain
> Cash, Paul S., Captain
> Houston, Samuel H., Captain
> Stegall, Harry E. Jr., 2nd Lt.

Co. I, NCNG, Newton, N. C. (Federally Recognized 23 April 1947)
> Wanzer, Charles R., Captain
> Barham, Jackson T., 1st Lt.
> Barringer, Jack E., 1st Lt.
> Taylor, William E., 1st Lt.
> Lutz, William H., 2nd Lt.

Co. K, NCNG, Gastonia, N. C. (Federally Recognized 24 July 1947)
> Harris, William F., Captain
> Armstrong, William B., 1st Lt.
> Dover, Harvey L., 1st Lt.
> Haas, Carter S., 1st Lt.
> Ratchford, Charles N., 2nd Lt.

REPORT OF THE ADJUTANT GENERAL   135

Co. L, NCNG, Morganton, N. C. (Federally Recognized 14 July 1947)

    Wiltshire, John L., Captain
    Bigham, Robert W., 1st Lt.
    Walker, Charles W., 1st Lt.
    Baker, Frank M., 2nd Lt.
    Lambeth, Donald C., 2nd Lt.
    White, Claude N. Jr., 2nd Lt.
    McCarter, Oscar G., WOJG

Co. M, NCNG, Shelby, N. C. (Federally Recognized 10 March 1947)

    Cabaniss, Robert E., Captain
    Scoggins, William C. Jr., 1st Lt.
    Stegall, Robert L., 2nd Lt.

112th FA Bn

Hq Hq Btry, NCNG, Lenoir, N. C. (Federally Recognized 9 June 1947)

    Forehand, Roy W., Lt. Colonel
    Seehorn, Theodore R., Major
    Rader, Ervin D., Captain
    Smith, Boone E., Captain
    Smith, Hal H., Captain
    Swanson, Garland W., Captain
    Tuttle, Robert H., Captain
    Underdown, Sidney L., Captain
    Hartley, Harold W., 1st Lt.
    Morgan, Raymond L., 1st Lt.
    Poteat, George W., 1st Lt.
    Robbins, Lawrence N., 1st Lt.
    Walker, Newland E., 1st Lt.
    Daughterty, Boyd R., 2nd Lt.
    Silver, Leon S., 2nd Lt.
    Beach, James W., WOJG
    Icenhour, Dewey R. Jr., WOJG

Service Btry, NCNG, Lenoir, N. C. (Federally Recognized 26 October 1948)

    Beach, Darwin E., 1st Lt.
    Setzer, Benjamin R., 2nd Lt.
    Harless, James C., CWO
    Rhodes, Lloyd G., WOJG

Btry. A, NCNG, Forest City, N. C. (Federally Recognized 14 November 1947)

    Bradley, Grover H., Captain
    Kichinke, Michael N. III, 1st Lt.
    Peeler, William B., 1st Lt.
    McDaniel, James H., 2nd Lt.
    Philbeck, Wade L., 2nd Lt.

Btry. B, NCNG, Spindale, N. C. (Federally Recognized 13 November 1947)

    Green, Herman E., Captain
    Padgett, Max, 1st Lt.
    Wilkie, Hubert G., 1st Lt.
    Henson, Amos G., 2nd Lt.
    Tomblin, Charles T., 2nd Lt.
    Harper, Fred T., WOJG

Btry, C, NCNG, North Wilkesboro, N. C. (Federally Recognized 3 February 1948)

    Boldin, Ralph A., Captain
    Thomas, William S. Jr., 1st Lt.
    Denton, Robert H., 2nd Lt.
    Shook, Clyde R., 2nd Lt.
    Wiles, Clarence D., 2nd Lt.
    Absher, Alton L., WOJG

113th FA Bn

Hq Hq Btry., NCNG, Louisburg, N. C. (Federally Recognized 28 August 1947)

    Yarborough, Edward F., Lt. Colonel
    McKinne, Collin, Major
    Perry, Darrell L., Major
    Daniel, Justice G., Captain
    Denning, James W., Captain
    Holmes, Melvin C., Captain
    Pearce, Philip D., Captain
    East, Thomas F., 1st Lt.
    Griffin, William S. Jr., 1st Lt.
    Ayscue, Jack E., 2nd Lt.
    Fuller, Kenneth A., 2nd Lt.
    Morton, Willard D., CWO

Service Btry., NCNG, Youngsville, N. C. (Federally Recognized 18 August 1947)

    Brown, Wiley, 1st Lt.
    Dickens, Lucius H. II, 2nd Lt.
    Hill, Robert C., 2nd Lt.
    Cheatham, Robert E., CWO
    Weathers, Jasper W., Jr., WOJG

Btry. A, NCNG, Zebulon, N. C. (Federally Recognized 27 July 1949)

    Davis, Barrie S., Captain
    Hinds, George H., 1st Lt.
    Potter, James M. Jr., 1st Lt.
    Finch, Foster D. Jr., 2nd Lt.
    Tippett, Jack M., 2nd Lt.

Btry. B, NCNG, Dunn, N. C. (Federally Recognized 10 November 1947)
Hall, Francis W., 1st Lt.
Wade, Edward H., 1st Lt.

Btry. C, NCNG, Roxboro, N. C. (Federally Recognized 9 April 1948)
Yeaman, James G., Captain
Wright, Wallace L., 1st Lt.
Hicks, Willie B., 2nd Lt.
Gentry, Ollie P., WOJG

130th AAA Bn (AW) (SP)

Hq Hq Btry, NCNG, Red Springs, N. C. (Federally Recognized 10 June 1947)
Lamont, William Jr., Lt. Col.
Dickson, Paul, Major
Lester, Thomas B. Jr., Major
Bullock, Walter R., Captain
McLean, Herbert S. Jr., Captain
Brock, Jimmy W., 1st Lt.
McMillan, Harvey F., 1st Lt.
Sighel, Norman C., CWO
McMillan, Charles P., WOJG

Btry. A, NCNG, Raeford, N. C. (Federally Recognized 10 March 1947)
English, Talmadge, 1st Lt.
Newton, Edwin D., 1st Lt.
Poole, William L. Jr, 1st Lt.
Macko, Thomas M., 2nd Lt.
Smith, Eugene P., 2nd Lt.
Dixon, Roger W., WOJG

Btry. B, NCNG, St. Pauls, N. C. ((Federally Recognized 8 November 1949)
Powers, Russell H., Captain
Sugar, Leon, 2nd Lt.
Sugar, Stanly, 2nd Lt.
Sherrill, Joe E. Jr., WOJG

Btry. C, NCNG, Sanford, N. C. (Federally Recognized 11 June 1948)
Staton, William W., Captain
Smith, Billie C., 1st Lt.
Winders, Gilbert L. Jr., 1st Lt.
McDonald, Thomas W., WOJG

Btry. D, NCNG, Southern Pines, N. C. (Federally Recognized 7 October 1949)
Wilson, William J., Captain
Horner, Ralph L., 1st Lt.
Irvin, James L., 1st Lt.
Kushner, Melvin, 2nd Lt.
Forsyth, Lennox, WOJG

252nd AAA Group, NCNG, Wilmington, N. C. (Federally Recognized 10 February 1948)

Corbett, Kenneth M., Colonel
Cobb, William A., Lt. Col.
Boylan, Joseph E. Jr., Major
Brown, Michael C., Major
Farmer, John E., Major
Reid, Henry V., Major
Cantwell, Robert C. III, Captain
Primrose, Hugh W., Captain
Smith, Arthur T., Captain
Walls, Osborne K., Captain
Herring, Oscar C., 1st Lt.
Bowden, Laurence O., 2nd Lt.
Crabtree, Purvis G., 2nd Lt.
Lanier, Homer A., 2nd Lt.
Orrell, Ernest C., CWO
Buck, Robert B., WOJG
Jeb Lee, John P. Jr., WOJG
Kelly, William J., WOJG
King, Adolph L. Jr., WOJG
Proctor, Grady M., WOJG
Williams, Russell C. Jr., WOJG

725th AAA AW Bn

Hq Hq Btry, NCNG, Whiteville, N. C. (Federally Recognized 10 January 1950)

Bowles, David A., Major
Brooks, James A., Major
Maultsby, Alexander, Major
Maultsby, John C., Major
Powell, Walter H. Jr., Captain
Waldron, Harold A., Captain
Dickens, Wallace J., 1st Lt.
Hickman, James B., 1st Lt.
Maxwill, James R., 1st Lt.
Rooks, Robert O., CWO
FormyDuval, John M., WOJG

Btry. A, NCNG, Shallotte, N. C. (Federally Recognized 28 November 1949)

Burns, John K., Captain
Carmichael, David B., 1st Lt.
Holden, Kemp R., 1st Lt.
Sellers, William T., 1st Lt.

Btry. B, NCNG, Fair Bluff, N. C. (Federally Recognized 1 May 1950)

Enzor, Simeon T., Captain
Collins, Lawrence O., 1st Lt.
Scott, Jimmie A., 1st Lt.
Rogers, Ed. F. Jr., WOJG

REPORT OF THE ADJUTANT GENERAL   139

Btry. C, NCNG, Bladenboro, N. C. (Federally Recognized 17 January 1950)
> Britt, David L., Captain
> Bullard, Johnnie G., 1st Lt.
> Stevens, Bennie E., 1st Lt.
> Cook, Andrew G., 2nd Lt.
> Lewis, Robert J. Sr., WOJG

Btry. D, NCNG, Benson, N. C. (Federally Recognized 14 April 1952)
> Willson, William W., 1st Lt.
> Chesnutt, Norwood B. Jr., 2nd Lt.
> Lucus, Herman H., WOJG

IV Corps Arty, NCNG, Charlotte, N. C. (Federally Recognized 9 October 1950)
> Griffin, Edward F., Brig. General
> Guthrie, Kermit L., Colonel
> Purvis, John A., Lt. Col.
> Ewing, William C., Major
> Friddle, George H., Major
> Gibbs, Wallace D. Jr., Major
> St. George, William M., Major
> Thompson, Lonnie F., Major
> Byrum, Porter B., Captain
> Garland, James B., Captain
> Isom, Charles D. Jr., Captain
> Kirkman, Guilford M., Captain
> Manning, James T., Captain
> Shaw, Victor, Jr., Captain
> Adeimy, Thomas E., 1st Lt.
> Connor, James W., 1st Lt.
> Cooper, George W., 1st Lt.
> Haubenreiser, Robert J., 1st Lt.
> Huggins, John S., 1st Lt.
> Crosland, John Jr., 2nd Lt.
> Huggins, Jimmie B., 2nd Lt.
> Gantt, Max P., 2nd Lt.
> Morse, Harris A., 2nd Lt.
> Johnson, Brooks R., WOJG

121st AAA Operations Det. NCNG, Charlotte, N. C. (Federally Recognized 14 Dec. 1951)
> Boone, Benjamin K., Major
> Sproles, James W., 1st Lt.

196th FA Group, NCNG, Wilmington, N. C. (Federally Recognized 10 February 1948)
> Willis, Weston H., Colonel
> Langston, Guy C., Lt. Col.
> Kornegay, Joseph T., Major

Ward, Clement M. Jr., Major
Bell, Richard K., Captain
Davis, James F., Captain
Dupree, Louis J. Jr., Captain
Glover, Murrell K., Captain
Simmons, Thomas W., Captain
Thompson, Robert L. Jr., Captain
Tart, Clarence C. Jr., 1st Lt.
Redmond, Franklin P., 1st Lt.
Thompson, William M., 1st Lt.
Waters, William G. Jr., 1st Lt.
Hoffman, Henry A., 2nd Lt.
Masters, Norman E., 2nd Lt.
Maxwill, William G., 2nd Lt.
Minor, William R., 2nd Lt.
Crary, Earnest F., CWO
Bourdas, Alexander, WOJG
McLawhorn, Charles H., WOJG
Sugg, Charles F., WOJG

252nd FA Group, NCNG, Grenesboro, N. C. (Federally Recognized 2 November 1950)

Wrenn, Oscar I., Colonel
Brown, Thomas E., Lt. Colonel
Compton, Carl S., Major
Gerringer, Linley W. Jr., Major
Poole, Frank R., Jr., Major
Taylor, Raleigh C. Jr., Major
Wannamaker, Charles W. Jr., Major
Carlton, Philip R. Jr., Captain
Groome, William A., Captain
Guard, Bruce C., 2nd Lt.
Routh, June E., 2nd Lt.
Jones, George S., CWO

505th FA Bn

Hq Hq Btry 505th FA Bn, NCNG, Greensboro, N. C. (Federally Recognized 28 April 1947)

Carruthers, Joseph T. Jr., Lt. Colonel
Brandt, Leon J. Jr., Major
Root, Hardy S., Major
Mitchell, Fillmore I. Jr., Captain
Thompson, Zane F., Captain
Williams, Hugh B., Captain
Chalmers, Carl M., 1st Lt.
Mallard, Walter W. Jr., 1st Lt.
Cobb, Ralph L., 2nd Lt.
Cates, John B., WOJG

Service Btry, NCNG, Greensboro, N. C. (Federally Recognized 2 December 1948)
>   Smith, Clarence D., 1st Lt.
>   Bateman, Robert M., CWO
>   Cooke, Charles L., WOJG
>   Hitchcock, Walter D., WOJG

Med Det, NCNG, Greensboro, N. C. (Federally Recognized 24 October 1949)
>   Reid, William J., Captain

Btry A, NCNG, Greensboro, N. C. (Federally Recognized 8 July 1948)
>   Pinnix, James C., 1st Lt.
>   McSweeney, James P., 2nd Lt.
>   Williams, Thomas F. Jr., 2nd Lt.
>   Tesh, Robert L., WOJG

Btry B, NCNG, Greensboro, N. C. (Federally Recognized 11 October 1949)
>   Gibson, Belton H. Jr., Captain
>   Gourley, Willard A. Jr., 2nd Lt.
>   Lewis, Kenneth E., 2nd Lt.
>   Yow, Clarence L., WOJG

Btry C, NCNG, Greensboro, N. C. (Federally Recognized 17 November 1950)
>   King, Hurley D., 1st Lt.
>   Smith, Ira A., 2nd Lt.
>   Wall, James A., 2nd Lt.
>   Hutson, Edward A., WOJG

167th MP Bn

Hq Hq Co, NCNG, Ahoskie, N. C. (Federally Recognized 26 February 1951)
>   Peterson, Bernice A., Lt. Colonel
>   Blythe, Joseph D., Major
>   Modlin, Morton S., Major
>   Bennett, Columbus L., Captain
>   Beasley, Carroll W., 2nd Lt.
>   Best, Edward P., 2nd Lt.
>   Norville, Herbert C. Jr., 2nd Lt.
>   Stanley, Howard T., 2nd Lt.
>   Guttu, Frank, WOJG
>   Pierce, John N., WOJG
>   Smith, Harry L., WOJG

Co. A, NCNG, Windsor, N. C. (Federally Recognized 26 February 1951)
>   Spruill, Charles B., Captain
>   Morris, Ben J., 2nd Lt.
>   Pierce, Melvin E., 2nd Lt.
>   Thomas, John P., 2nd Lt.

Co. B, NCNG, Lasker, N. C. (Federally Recognized 10 April 1952)
> Beale, Walter H. Jr., 1st Lt.
> Draper, Calvin T., 2nd Lt.
> Hassell, Jack A., 2nd Lt.
> Powers, Michael F., 2nd Lt.
> Wiggins, Robert M., 2nd Lt.

540th FA Bn (NGUS)

Hq Hq Btry, NCNG, High Point, N. C. (Federally Recognized 3 November 1952)
> Lee, John H., Lt. Colonel
> Guyer, Homer D. Jr., 1st Lt.
> Hodgin, David A., 1st Lt.

Btry A, NCNG, High Point, N. C. (Federally Recognized 3 November 1952)
> Lloyd, Joseph M., 1st Lt.
> Regan, Joseph C., 2nd Lt.
> Blackwill, Rudolph, WOJG

123rd Signal Radar Maint. Unit, Type C, NCNG, Wilmington, N. C. (Federally Recognized 24 January 1951)
> Casey, Jephthah Jr., WOJG

217th RCAT Det, NCNG, Raleigh, N. C. (Federally Recognized 7 February 1951)
> Smith, Kerr H., 2nd Lt.

3624th Ord Med Maint Co, NCNG, Butner, N. C. (Federally Recognized 20 February 1948)
> Davis, Louie H., Captain
> Fletcher, James M., 1st Lt.
> Kubachko, Andrew Jr., 1st Lt.
> Ferrell, Arthur E., CWO
> Davis, Stuart M., WOJG
> Lemons, Arthur L., WOJG

Hq Hq & Svc Co 378th Engr. (C) Bn (NGUS) (Federally Recognized
> Neel, Tally M., Lt. Colonel
> Battley, William R., Major

Co. A. 378th Engr. (C) Bn (NGUS) (Federally Recognized
> Beam, Leslie B. Jr., 1st Lt.
> Craig, Robert H., 1st Lt.

Co. B, 378th Engr. (C) Bn (NGUS) Federally Recognized
> Robbins, Clontz, 1st Lt.

Co. C, 378th Engr. (C) Bn (NGUS) (Federally Recognized
> Suther, Carrloll, 1st Lt.

REPORT OF THE ADJUTANT GENERAL

AIR UNITS

Hq, NC ANG, Charlotte, N. C.

    Payne, William J., Lt. Col.
    Brooks, Robert W. Jr., Major
    Jetton, Sidney L., Major
    Harding, Frederic D., Major
    Byrd, Henry C., Lt.. Col.

156th Ftr. Bomber Sq. NCANG, Charlotte, N. C.

    Nantz, Kenneth E., CWO(W-2)
    Shelden, Howard W., Captain
    Hunt, Marvin R., 2nd Lt.
    Raeford, James W., 1st Lt.
    Hipp, Wilton L., 1st Lt.
    Higgins, Robert G., Major
*   Hanes, Charlie M., Captain
    Griffith, Edward C., 1st Lt.
    White, Earl W., Captain
    Foster, Frank H., Captain

263rd Comm. Sq. Opn., NC ANG, Wadesboro, N. C. (Federally Recognized 3 November 1952)

    Tyson, John K., 1st Lt.
    McCaskill, Harry L., 2nd Lt.

OFFICE OF THE SENIOR ARMY INSTRUCTOR
NORTH CAROLINA NATIONAL GUARD
POST OFFICE BOX 791
RALEIGH, NORTH CAROLINA

Year Ending 1951   1 January 1952

STATION LIST

Station	Office Address	Mail Address	Phone
AHOSKIE Maj. G. J. Flynn, Jr. 0397768 Adv. 167th MP Bn. SFC J. F. Conner, RA 34089841 Sgt. Instr. 167th MP Bn.	Ahoskie Bank Building	P. O. Box 91	386
ASHEBORO Capt. Wilson A. Hayden 02017055 (Delay enroute to join) Instr. 2nd Bn. 120th Inf.			
BUTNER Lt. Col. O. J. Ferrill 0444896 Ord. Tech Adv. M. Sgt. B. J. Lester RA 15040775 Sgt. Instr. 3624th Ord. MM Co.	NC NG Maint. Pool	NC NG Maint. Pool	Creedmore 3511
CLINTON Maj. Earl Lynch 0450386 Adv. 3rd Bn. 119th Inf. SFC J. E. Reichard RA 7021292 Sgt. Instr., 3rd Bn. 119th Inf.	Lee Building Main Street	P. O. Box 772	3225
CANTON Maj. R. E. Anderson 01634801 Adv. 30th Sig. Co.	NG Armory	P. O. Box 774	None
CHARLOTTE Lt. Col. I. G. Walz 028876 Instr. IV Corps Arty M. Sgt. J. C. Henderson RA 6970619 Sgt. Instr. IV Corps Arty. SFC C. W. Burnett RA 34174514 Adm Asst. to IV Corps Arty Instr.	127 W 7th St.	127 W 7th St.	5-3893
DURHAM Maj. J. N. Schoming 044755 Instr. 119th Inf. M. Sgt. M. E. Curtis RA 20533744 Adm. Asst. to 119th Inf. Instr. M. Sgt. P. G. Manning RA 14018289 Sgt. Instr. 119th Inf.	302 Morris St.	302 Morris St.	3-9555
GREENSBORO Lt. Col. A. Emmerson 0100813 Adv. 252d FA Gp. and 505th FA Bn. M. Sgt. A. E. McLean RA 39604996 Adm. Asst. to 252d FA Gp. Instr. SFC P. W. Lebeau RA 206 15490 Sgt. Instr. 252d FA Gp.	Rm. 36b P. O. Bldg.	P. O. Box 2035	4-3028

REPORT OF THE ADJUTANT GENERAL 145

Station	Office Address	Mail Address	Phone
HENDERSON			
Capt. J. L. Spratt 039233 Instr. 1st Bn. 119th Inf. SFC D. L. Williams RA 16015361 Sgt. Instr. 1st Bn. 119th Inf.	Armory	P. O. Box 748	951-J
LENOIR			
Maj. J. W. Fielder 033842 Instr. 112th FA Bn. M. Sgt. R. W. Hood RA 6666320 Sgt. Instr. 112 FA Bn.	Rm. 304 Duke Power Bldg.	P. O. Box 721	1140
LOUISBURG			
Lt. Col. A. C. Ball 032070 Instr. 113th FA Bn. Sgt. E. D. Frank RA 209 27454 Sgt. Instr. 113th FA Bn.	NG Armory	P. O. Box 122	308-6
NEW BERN			
M. Sgt. J. H. Dease RA 14009273 Adm. Assist. to 196th FA Gp. Instr. (To be transferred to Kinston, N. C.)	Rm. 308 P. O. Bldg.	P. O. Box 929	4618
RAEFORD			
WOJG W. E. Marlar W2145720	Hoke County Office Bldg.	P.O. Box 576	None
RALEIGH			
Col L. C. Bizzell 010250 Senior Army Instructor Capt. I . V. Hester 0529837 Army Avn. Adv-Instr. CWO J. B. Liles W903425 Adm. Assistant CWO J. T. Shurling W903816 Adm. Assistant M. Sgt. B. B. Smith RA 6376333 Sgt.-Major M. Sgt. F. J. Skufoa RA 6744595 Stenographer M. Sgt. C. B. Martin RA 34087058 Supply & File Section Sgt. W. H. Stephenson RA 34813128 Message & Publication Section Sgt. Joel Martinez Army Airplane Mechanic Sgt. R. A. Hendrickson NG 15252692 Message Center, NCMD	Rms. 12-15 Justice Bldg.	P. O. Box 791	4-3611 Ext 513
Col. H. H. Harris 011817 Instr. 30th Inf. Div. M. Sgt. Ward D. Greeno RA 3703176.0 Sgt. Instr., 30th Inf Div.	Rm. 408 Masonic Temple Bldg.	Rm. 408 Masonic Temple Bldg.	3-4977

Station	Office Address	Mail Address	Phone

SALISBURY

Maj. T. A. Hopkins 036057
Instr. 120th Inf.
SFC Q. L. Johnson, Sr. RA 14001806
Sgt. Instr. 120th Inf.
M. Sgt. J. P. Whitecavage RA 13100781
Sgt. Instr. 2d Bn. 120th Inf.
Sgt. C. H. Clark RA 37690617
Adm. Asst. to 120th Inf.

113 W Concil St.   P. O. Box 97   4186

SHELBY

Capt. S. Y. Moore 01300685
Adv. 3rd Bn., 120th Inf.

Weathers Blanton Bldg. 205 S. Washington St.   P. O. Box 249   7141

WHITEVILLE

Maj. F. W. Shelton 033612
Instr. 725th AAA AW Bn. (M)
SFC J. W. Highsmith RA 6969137
Sgt. Instr. 725th AAA AW Bn. (M)
M. Sgt. E. F. Noland RA 6942368
Sgt. Instr. 725th AAA AW Bn. (M) (Delay enroute to Join)

NG Armory   P. O. Box 673   299-R

WILMINGTON

Col. F. L. Van Atta 0267544
Adv. 252 AAA Gp.
SFC J. B. Knight RA 44136752
Adm. Assist. to 252d AAA Gp. Adv.

Rm.14 P. O. Bldg.   P. O. Box 1018   3-1125

WILSON

Maj. J. H. Ratliff, Jr. 0450503
Adv. 2d Bn. 119th Inf.
SFC R. M. Staley RA 6971923
Sgt. Instr. 2nd Bn. 119th Inf.

Rms. 616-617 Nat'l Bank Building   P. O. Box 249   6189

WINSTON-SALEM

SFC M. E. Poinsett RO 17274487
Sgt. Instr. 1st Bn. 120th Inf.

620½ W 4th St.   P. O. Box 3117   4-9621

DISTRIBUTION

A B C M
Maj. Donavan
Capt. York
M. Sgt. Boyd, NCMD
Miss Duke, NCMD
Lt. Carter

OFFICE OF THE SENIOR ARMY INSTRUCTOR
NORTH CAROLINA NATIONAL GUARD
POST OFFICE BOX 791
RALEIGH, NORTH CAROLINA

Year Ending 1952   1 January 1953

STATION LIST

Station	Office Address	Mail Address	Phone
AHOSKIE Maj. G. J. Flynn, Jr. 0397768 Adv. 167th MP Bn. SFC J. F. Conner RA3408941 Sgt. Instr. 167th MP Bn.	Ahoskie Bank Bldg.	P. O. Box 91	2824
ASHEBORO Capt. W. A. Hayden 02017055 Adv. 2nd Bn. 120th Inf. M. Sgt. J. P. Whitecavage RA13100781 Sgt. Instr. 2nd Bn. 120th Inf. M. Sgt. K. M. France RA6886739 Sgt. Instr. 2nd 120th Inf.	Rm. 202 Griffin Clinic S Fayetteville St.	P. O. Box 347	5050
BUTNER M. Sgt. R. H. Deetz RO6660471 Ord. Tech NCO NCNG & Sgt. Instr. 3624th Ord. (Direct Support) Co.	State Maint. Pool Butner, N. C.	State Maint. Pool Butner, N. C.	3511 (Creedmore)
CANTON Capt. W. O. Torgerson 01633599 Adv. Sig. Co., 30th Inf. Div. & Tech. Adv. to all units having signal epuipment M. Sgt. L. R. Bishop RA6957484 Sgt. Instr. Sig. Co., 30th Inf. Div.	NG Armory	P. O. Box 1002	2877
CHARLOTTE (1) SFC C. W. Burnett RO34174514 Admin. Assist. to IV Corps Arty & 121st AAA O'pn Det. Instr.	101 N. Graham St.	101 N. Graham St.	5-3893
CHARLOTTE (2) M. Sgt. O. F. Anderson RA20412152 Sgt. Instr. 378th Engr. (C) Bn. NGUS	NG Armory Cecil St.	P. O. Box 4100	56939
CLINTON SFC. C. D. Swick RA35784234 Sgt. Instr. 3rd Bn., 119th Inf.	Lee Bldg. Main St.	P. O. Box 772	3225
DURHAM Lt. Col. W. C. Sharp 031408 Inst. 119th Inf. M. Sgt. H. E. Allen RA6662371 Sgt. Instr. 119th Inf. M. Sgt. M. E. Curtis RA20533774 Admin. Assist. to 119th Inf. Inst. SFC C. F. Herron RA15408930 Admin. Asst. to 119th Inf. Instr.	302 Morris St.	302 Morris St.	3-9555

Station	Office Address	Mail Address	Phone
GREENSBORO			
M. Sgt. J. W. Hall RA14198904 Sgt. Instr. 252d FA Gp. 505th FA Bn.	Rm. 36b P. O. Bldg.	P. O. Box 2035	4-3028
SFC R. C. Hinkle RA13211677 Admin. Asst. to 252d FA Gp. Instr.			
HENDERSON			
Maj. E. C. Navarre 0404332 Adv. 1st. Bn. 119th Inf. SFC D. L. Williams RA16015361 Sgt. Instr. 1st Bn., 119th Inf.	508 S. Chestnut St.	P. O. Box 748	7363
HIGH POINT			
M. Sgt. A. J. Kilgariff RO13004772 Sgt. Instr. 540th FA Bn. NGUS.	NG Armory	306 W. Ray St.	None
KINSTON			
M. Sgt. H. L. Lindsey RA34084005 Admin. Asst. to 196th FA Gp. Instr.	NG Armory	306 N. Heritage St.	5962
LENOIR			
Maj. J. W. Fielder 033842 Instr. 112th FA Bn., IV Corps Arty. & 121st AAA Opn Det. M. Sgt. R. W. Hood RA666320 Sgt. Instr., 112th FA Bn.	Armory Annex	P. O. Box 721	4-3723
LOUISBURG			
Lt. Col. A. C. Ball 032070 Instr. 113th FA Bn., 196th FA Gp., 252d FA Gp., 505th FA Bn., & 540th FA Bn. SFC C. R. Slate RA7001833 Sgt. Instr. 113th FA Bn.	NG Armory	P. O. Box 122	8481
RAEFORD			
Capt. R. P. DeWitt 01058225' Adv. 130th AAA AW Bn. SFC J. B. Knight RA44136752 Admin. Asst. to 130th AAA Bn. Adv.	NG Armory	P. O. Box 396	None
RALEIGH			
Col. W. R. Watson 08354 Senior Army Instr. Maj. L. R. Cantlebary 060350 Army Avn. Adv.-Instr. & 217th AAA Det. (RCAT) CWO J. B. Liles W903425 Admin. Asst. M. Sgt. E. J. Browne RO15016238 Sgt.-Major M. Sgt. W. D. Greene RA37031760 Sgt. Instr.	Rms. 12-15 Justice Bldg.	P. O. Box 791	4-3611 Ext-513

REPORT OF THE ADJUTANT GENERAL 149

Station	Office Address	Mail Address	Phone
RALEIGH (Continued)			
M. Sgt. C. B. Martin RA34087058			
Supply & File Section			
SFC W. H. Stephenson RA34813128			
Message and Publication Section			
SFC Joel Martinez RA18047602			
Army Airplane Mechanic			
Sgt. L. V. Earp RA6934029			
Stenographer			
Sgt. J. R. Griffin RA34644462			
Admin Asst.			
SALISBURY			
Maj. T. A. Hopkins 036057	Rm. 209	P. O. Box 97	4186
Instr. 120th Inf.	P. O. Bldg.		
M. Sgt. W. K. Leach RA20466854			
Sgt. Instr. 120th Inf.			
SFC C. H. Clark RA3790617			
Admin. Asst. to 120th Inf. Instr.			
SHELBY			
Capt. S. Y. Moore 01300685	Weather	P. O. Box	7141
Adv. 3d 120th Inf.	Blanton	249	
SFC J. Holland RA14149592	Bldg. 205		
Sgt. Instr. 3d Bn. 120th Inf.	S. Washington St.		
TARBORO			
Maj. C. R. Howard 01290250	125 E.	125 E.	2727
Adv. 2d Bn., 119th Inf.	St. James St.	St. James St.	
M. Sgt. G. T. Jackson RA44202021			
Sgt. Instr. 2d Bn., 119th Inf.			
WHITEVILLE			
Maj. F. W. Shelton 033612	NG Armory	P. O. Box	299R
Instr. 725th AAA AW Bn. (M)		673	
252d AAA Gp., & 123d SRMU			
M. Sgt. E. F. Nolan RA6942368			
Sgt. Instr. 725th AAA AW Bn. (M)			
WILMINGTON			
(No Personnel Assigned)	Rm. 14		None
	P. O. Bldg.		
WINSTON-SALEM			
Capt. H. C. Hammer 02006325	Rm. 210	P. O. Box	4-9621
Adv. 1st Bn., 120th Inf.	P. O. Bldg.	3117	
SFC H. H. Haywood RA38059511			
Sgt. Instr. 1st Bn., 120th Inf.			

KNOWN GAINS

Schaefer, John A.,	SFC	RA33199444	ETA 7 Jan. 53	EDCSA 23 Dec. 52

KNOWN LOSSES

Slate, Clyde R.,	SFC	RA7001833	ETD 10 Jan. 53	EDCSA 10 Jan. 53
Smith, Bishop B.,	M. Sgt.	RO6376333	ETD1 Dec. 52	EDCSA 20 Jan. 53
Knight, Joseph B.,	SFC	RA44136752	ETD	EDCSA 20 Jan. 53
Martin, Clyde B.,	M. Sgt.	RA34087058	ETD	EDCSA 10 Feb. 53
Whitecavage, J. P.,	M. Sgt.	RA13100781	EDT	EDCSA 10 Feb. 53
Moore, Sam Y.,	Capt.	0130685	ETD Feb. 53	

REPORT OF THE ADJUTANT GENERAL

OFFICE OF THE ADJUTANT GENERAL
NORTH CAROLINA NATIONAL GUARD
RALEIGH, N. C.

Report of Proceedings of Board of Officers

Proceedings of a Board of Officers which convened at Raleigh, North Carolina pursuant to Par. 2, Special Orders No. 106, State of North Carolina, Adjutant General's Department, 12 March 1952, copy of which is attached as Exhibit A.

The Board met pursuant to the foregoing order at Raleigh, North Carolina at 0930 12 March 1952.

Members present:
Major General John H. Manning, The Adjutant General, North Carolina
Brigadier General Claude T. Bowers, Commanding General, 30th Infantry Division, NCNG
Colonel Lee C. Bizzell, Senior Army Instructor, North Carolina National Guard

PURPOSE:

To select the unit of the North Carolina National Guard to receive the Eisenhower Trophy for 1951, in accordance with the provisions of Section VI, NGR 44, dated 6 September 1951.

FINDINGS:

The Board found that the **Service Battery, 112th FA Battalion**, NCNG, met the specifications listed in Paragraph 33, Section VI, NGR 44, dated 6 Sept 1951.

RECOMMENDATIONS:

The Board recommends that the **Service Battery, 112th FA Battalion**, North Carolina National Guard, be awarded the Eisenhower Trophy **for the year 1951.**

The Board adjourned at 1000 12 March 1952.

JOHN H. MANNING
Major General, NCNG
President

CLAUDE T. BOWERS
Brigadier General, 30 Inf Div, NCNG
Member

LEE C. BIZZELL
Colonel, Inf, RA
Recorder

EISENHOWER TROPHY (ARMY).—a. Reference is made to Section VI, NGR 44, dated 6 September 1951.

A board of officers appointed in accordance with reference cited in Par. a, above, has recommended to the Chief, National Guard Bureau that **Tank Company, 119th Infantry (90 MM Gun)**, NCNG, be named as winner of subject trophy for calendar year 1952.

Other units which met all requirements are as follows:

123rd Signal Detachment (Radar Maint. Unit, Type C)
94th Army Band
Company M, 119th Infantry
Service Btry, 113th FA Bn.
Hq Hq Co, 2nd Bn, 120th Infantry

Tank Company, 119th Infantry (90 MM Gun) and each of the other units listed are commended for attaining an excellent record during 1952 and it is expected that even more units will be eligible for consideration for this award during 1953.

THIRD ARMY NATIONAL GUARD TRAINING TROPHY (ARMY).—a. Reference is made to Par. 5, Sec. III, NC NG Bulletin No. 6, dated 22 February 1952.

Hq, Third Army, has advised this department that **Btry B, 113th FA Bn** NCNG, Dunn, N. C., has been declared winner of the Third Army National Guard Training Trophy for **calendar year 1951** based on nominations submitted by State Adjutants General of the Third Army Area. Listed below are the positions of other units nominated within this Army Area.

State	Unit	Rating
South Carolina	Service Battery, 178th Field Artillery Battalion	92.84
Florida	Tank Company (M), 124th Infantry	89.12
Tennessee	Company A, 173d Armored Calvery Regiment	87.66
Georgia	Hq. & Hq. Btry., 950th AAA AW Battalion	84.23
Mississippi	3656th Ordinance Medium Maintenance Company	79.08
Alabama	Negative Report	

It is tentatively planned that the trophy will be presented by the Army Commander or his representative at the unit's home station on 28 April 1952. The officers and men of Btry B, 113th FA Bn are commended for having achieved this outstanding accomplishment. Every unit of the North Carolina National Guard should make special effort beginning now to win this trophy during the current calendar year. Several units are already off to a good start in this direction, and each individual of these units should appoint himself a committee of one to see that every available opportunity is taken advantage of in order that when the points are computed at the end of the year his unit will be on top.

THIRD ARMY NATIONAL GUARD TRAINING TROPHY (ARMY).—a. References:

(1) Par. 7, Section I, Training Memorandum No. 1 (National Guard), Headquarters, Third Army, dated 1 January 1953.

(2) Par. 14, Section IV, NC NG Bulletin No. 1, 2 January 1953.

Based on reports submitted by Army Instructors, this Department in coordination with the Senior Army Instructor, NCNG, has selected the unit obtaining the highest rating for the Third Army Training Trophy based on criteria listed in reference a(1) above. Report has been submitted to Hq, Third Army, recommending that Btry B, 113th FA Bn, Dunn, N. C., with an average rating of 95.26%, be considered as the winner from this State in order that determination may be made as to the winner in the Third Army Area. Other units in this State receiving a percentage rating of 90 or above are as follows:

    Hq Hq Btry, 252nd AAA Gp, Wilmington, N. C.—92.81%
    Hq Hq Co, 2nd Bn, 119th Inf, Wilson, N. C.—91.56%

This is the second year in succession that Btry B, 113th FA Bn, has achieved the highest rating in this State for this trophy. This is truly an outstanding record, and it is sincerely hoped that this unit will be declared winner within the Third Army Area, as was the case for calendar year 1951. Other units listed above are commended for making a creditable showing, and all units are urged to begin making preparations now to win this trophy for calendar year 1953.

SPECIAL DUTY OF TROOPS

1951-1952...................None

ADJUTANTS GENERAL OF NORTH CAROLINA

(The Office of Adjutant General was created by Chapter XVIII, Section 7, of the Laws of 1806)

Name	County	Term
Benjamin Smith	Brunswick County	1806–1807
Edward Pasteur	Craven County	1807–1808
Calvin Jones	Wake County	1808–1812
Robert Williams	Surry County	1812–1821
Beverly Daniel	Wake County	1821–1840
Robert Williams Haywood	Wake County	1840–1857
Richard C. Cotten	Chatham County	1857–1860
John F. Hoke	Lincoln County	1860–1861
James G. Martin	U. S. Army, formerly of Pasquotank County	1861–1863
Daniel G. Fowle	Wake County	1863
Richard C. Gatlin	U. S. Army, formerly of Lenoir County	1864–1865
John A. Gilmer, Jr.	Guilford County	1866–1868
Abiel W. Fisher	Bladen County	1868–1872
John C. Gorman	Wake County	1872–1877
Johnstone Jones	Wake County	Jan. 1877–Dec. 1888
James Dodge Glenn	Guilford County	Jan. 1889–Dec. 1892
Francis H. Cameron	Wake County	1893–1896
Andrew D. Cowles	Iredell County	Feb. 1897–Dec. 1898
Beverly S. Royster	Granville County	Dec. 1898–Dec. 1904
Thomas R. Robertson	Mecklenburg County	Jan. 1905–Mar. 1909
Joseph F. Armfield	Iredell County	Apr. 1909–Oct. 1910
Roy L. Leinster	Iredell County	Nov. 1910–Aug. 1912
Gordon Smith	Wake County	Nov. 1912–Jan. 1913
Lawrence W. Young	Buncombe County	Jan. 1913–June 1916 Sept. 1917–Aug. 1918
Beverly S. Royster	Granville County	June 1916–Aug. 1917 Sept. 1918–June 1920
J. Van B. Metts	New Hanover County	June 1920–July 31, 1951
Thomas B. Longest (Actg.)	Wake County,(formerly Biscoe, Va.)	Aug. 1–Sept. 30, 1951
John Hall Manning	Durham County	Oct. 1, 1951–

CPSIA information can be obtained
at www.ICGtesting.com
Printed in the USA
BVHW041427220219
540923BV00007B/251/P